THE MAKING OF A WONDER WOMAN

Bonnie VanDeraa's Autobiography

Jana,

Thank you for being you. Thank you for supporting me through this. Remember that even in the darkest moments, you are still someone else's brightest light. I love you.

-Bonnie VanDeraa aka "Wonder Woman"

First published 2021 in the United States of America by

KDP Publishing

Bonnifersunshine@gmail.com

ISBN 978-0-578-83569-3

Copyright © 2021 Bonnie VanDeraa

Cover design by Cody Frusher

Frusher & Company

http://www.Frusherandcompany.com

DEDICATION

This book is dedicated to someone very special.

Someone who, without them, this book would not have happened.

It would have been impossible.

She took my scrambled brain with all of it's loose wires and "something something's" and turned them into sense and into a beauty that is unexplained.

Before her, I had trouble putting thoughts into words.

But yet, I knew I needed to write this book to help others.

Before her, writing thoughts on paper was nearly impossible.

But yet, this urgency grew within me to write.

Before her, my purpose was quickly vanishing. How would I write my story?

Then I met my speech therapist Juliana.

"Thank you" does not cover everything you have done for me. Some people may only come into your life for a moment, but in that brief moment, they forever change your life.

Forward

By Julie Sellmeyer

This reading is just a tiny glimpse into The Making of a Wonder Woman. By no means is this the full complete story.

To say my friend Bonnie is an inspiration doesn't seem like a big enough statement. She has never been a quitter nor someone who believes in the word "can't". She is fierce and determined. She pushes me and others just by being who she is Every Single Day.

She reminds us all to

Not give up,

Not give in,

Never stop fighting

For it's 5 minutes at a time.

It's a privilege to walk beside her in her life journey, literally and figuratively.

W.W. Sidekick aka Julie Sellmeyer

Making of a Wonder Woman

Table of Contents

THE MAKING OF A WONDER WOMAN INTRODUCTION

That day started out just like any other, but it had ended like no other. There I laid in that hospital bed fighting for my life. I had been shot in my head by the person I trusted most. I fought hard, so hard in fact, that the nurses began calling me "Wonder Woman". It stuck with my family and friends who visited me daily. They also began with the nickname. I awoke to being called "Wonder Woman" and smiled at the name. The nickname stuck even to this day.

The reason I chose the name "The Making of A Wonder Woman" as a title for this book is that it tells the story of how a little girl fought many many battles in life, then grew up to conquered the biggest battle that should have killed her yet, and continues to fight every single day onward. It shows how anyone who has determination can also be a superhero. It's encouragement for the soul. It's an example of grit, tenacity, being a fighter, a little sense of humor, and willingness to fight each battle with a fierceness. Remember!!!! Never give up, Never give in, for it's five minutes at a time.

Everywhere I go, I'm known as "Wonder Woman".....from my medical team to friends and family to my running/walking partners and fans. It's been an incredible journey. To me, it's been about encouraging and listening to others. When I'm walking a race, I always have people walk with me who tell me their own personal stories of battles won......beating cancer, knee surgeries, etc. Or they tell me that they almost dropped out of the race, but then saw me walking the race with my walker. Seeing me gave them encouragement and strength to carry on.

Even in the darkest moment in life, you are still someone's brightest light.

-BonniferWW

Chapter 1

The Real Incident

The day I died

The bullet hit.

I screamed. I cried.

The pain was incredible.

The darkness was swirling in.

I fought back, hard, and with everything I had.

I thought that was it, but no, it continued.

The bullet hit. AGAIN.

I screamed for it to stop.

I cried, for the pain was immense.

The darkness kept swirling in.

But I kept fighting back, hard, and with everything I had.

I thought that was it, but no, it continued.

Then came the baton stick over my head, guarded with my hands.

I yelled his name for him to stop.

I cried like never before.

That darkness again, still determined to win.

But I was still there more determined than ever to conquer.

I thought that was it, while it was, it also really wasn't.

That was it in a sense because that was when I died.

Bonnie died that moment.

The bright, chipper, full of sunshine her.

The hard working, caring, nonstop working paramedic.

The constantly giving of herself, pushing herself, crazy goofball type.

Oh, those were the days.

She died and is no longer.

Here I am.

I don't know who or what I am.

I don't know why or how long I am here for.

I do know I have a temper and get ugly at the drop of a hat.

I do know I get frustrated at stupid things.

I do know my attention and focus last about half a second.

So many more issues.

Now these are the days.

Here I am and this is my present.

I also have a grand purpose for my life!

I also know that I am well loved by hundreds.

I also know that I am well taken care of by oh so many.

I also know that ALL of my needs have been taken care of through this.

I do not walk this journey alone.

I have many by my side.

So please be patient with me.

I'm learning who this new person is.

I don't know her very well at all.

Sometimes I hate her.

Sometimes I wish I didn't know her at all.

Then I realize I am her and have no choice.

I must continue on.

I must continue to put one foot in front of the other.

I must continue forward.

There is no other choice.

Don't ever give in.

Don't ever give up.

For its five minutes at a time.

-Bonnifer WW

If you knew the exact date, time, and method of your death, how would that change the way you live your life? Or would you change anything at all? If you knew the same for someone you love dearly, would it change the way you loved them? If you knew the same for someone you didn't like so much, would you treat them differently?

On January 22, 2018, Mick came to my apartment and asked me to take him to the ER because he was suddenly blind in his left eye and he was having severe chest pain. Now, Mick was not a guy to go to a doctor and especially the ER unless he felt like he was almost dying. Otherwise, he was his own "doctor". If he needed stitches, he would stitch himself right up. When he stabbed himself in the abdomen while on the kill floor at the meat business his family had, he'd clean it and stitch it if need be. So, when he wanted to go to the ER, I was shocked and a bit nervous. Maybe even scared. We had worked together for two years on the ambulance, so he was like a big brother to me. He, and all the guys at the station referred to me as "little sis".

I drove us to St Francis Hospital in Vinita OK. It was where we took our ambulance patients too and hung out sometimes when not on calls. Mick and I would even help out in the ER for a bit when the nurses were slammed. It's difficult to drive a personal car as you're supposed to, you know…. the speed limit and such, when you have a family emergency especially when you are used to being in the ambulance. I concentrated on the road while also keeping an eye on Mick. He'd already taken 324mg aspirin prior to us leaving my apartment. Anyway, while I was driving, Mick called in and told them that we were coming and what was going on with him.

When we arrived, we went straight back on account of his severe chest pain. I could tell he was even scared. He was never scared. This made me even more anxious. Dr. C. did every possible test on Mick from CT and x-rays to many lab tests. Everything, yes everything came back normal. The medications Mick had been given though had gotten his pain under control and for that, I was very thankful for. Doc and the cardiologist wanted to keep Mick overnight for observation, but of course Mick refused. Doc wanted to send Mick to an optometrist in town and he did agree to go. Only thing is that when we got there, Mick changed his mind saying he wanted to go to his own eye doctor. He even asked me if that was okay. Of course, it was.

We went home. I could tell Mick was severely depressed, but when asked, he always said he was okay, at least when I asked him anyhow. He left saying he was going to go to the doctor. I only hoped he would really go.

Late that night, he stopped by again. He was drunk, like really drunk, but had prescription eye drops too. He stated that doc said that a blood vessel had popped, probably from stress, and it would be back to normal in a week or so. In my mind, it was a huge relief and I told him so. I was incredibly positive and encouraging. He was very down and depressed still. I told him we'd get through this together, that now we knew his heart was good, and now his vision would be okay in a few days too. Life would be okay.

But little did I know that life would be otherwise. This night was to be my last night of my normal life. He left after that. I didn't see him again until the next afternoon.

January 23rd, 2018 was the day that would forever change my life. He texted me asking if I needed anything to which I replied no, but just a reminder about the washer wasn't working. He texted back saying he would stop in shortly, say hi, and look at the washer. Okay fabulous!

A short while later, he stopped in. I was lying on the floor, on a pile of blankets, watching TV. It was a ridiculously small black and white TV, which was on the floor. Yes, I know.... get with the 21st century woman! I had no TV, and it was all he had available. So hey, it's better than nothing you smart mouth goofballs.

He entered and said hi. We talked for a minute. Then I went back to watching TV. I didn't take much notice of what he was doing. I heard him moving around and making a little noise, but it was really nothing to me. I assumed he was fixing to look at the washer.

I don't remember what show was on. I wish I did, but then it's probably better that I don't. I don't remember if it was a commercial or not. But I was lying there all relaxed when suddenly I was on my knees, holding my head, and screaming. For a minute, the echo was so loud in my head that I couldn't hear myself screaming. But then, when it quieted a bit, I did. Imagine the loudest you've ever screamed, whether it be on a roller coaster or screaming for help in a car wreck. This was still louder. I couldn't stop screaming. The pain was..............real. The pain was intense. The pain was on fire.

At first, I thought maybe Mick had a bad PTSD episode. I figured he'd probably throw me in his truck and drive me to the hospital. It was an accident, right? Things would be okay right? He surely didn't mean to do this. He was asking me questions like "What happened?", "Where'd the gun come from?", and "How'd the gun go off?".

I thought that was the end when it was actually just the beginning. Next thing I knew, I was screaming again, holding my head even tighter. It was Deja vu of the first shot. WHAT THE HELL! I knew now this was not an accident. He meant to be doing this. He was seriously trying to murder me. It was time to fight for my life now like I had never ever fought for anything before. Give it my all or die.

I knelt there trying to get my breath and figure out a plan to get out of this safely. I could feel the blood rolling down my hands and arms. I could smell my very own blood. I've smelled blood before, many times before in fact with the career I had, but to smell blood and know it's your own is completely different. It grabs your attention. You know you are about to die unless you do something immediately to change the matter.

Before I could think of anymore, I again began screaming with all I could muster praying that someone would please hear me and call for help. The whacks kept coming over and over again on top of my head. My hands were there protecting my head, but how much could my hands take and how long would they last? How much damage to my brain was this causing? All these thoughts flew through my head. I screamed at him to stop. I kept screaming at him to stop until he finally did. The baton stick had broken over my head.

I laid there, waiting for something else to happen. Another gunshot. Another beating. Something. What else would he do to me? I just laid still and sobbed. There was silence.

Nothing. Then he spoke. "I'm going to go call 911." That's all he said. Then I heard the door close. I couldn't breathe. Not in the sense of trauma, but in the sense of what if he came back in that door? What if he changed his mind? What if....?

I also knew that if I was going to survive, that I was sure not going to keep lying on this floor. I crawled around on the floor looking for my phone. I spent several seconds looking. I found out later that he had taken it with him.

I started to panic. How was I going to get help without my phone? I wasn't going to just lay down and die. Breathe Bonnie breathe. I realized there would most likely be neighbors home somewhere in the building, but I also realized the danger in going outside. Since he wanted me dead, he would not hesitate to shoot me again if he saw I was still alive.

I crawled to the front door and outside. I crawled backward down the steps. Still no one was outside. I was scared to call out for help. I could see the trail of blood I was leaving. It gave me motivation to keep moving. Just keep moving. Don't stop. Don't close your eyes. Don't lie down.

I made it to a neighbor's door where someone was almost always home. I knocked. A man answered and cussed when he saw me. I calmly asked him to call 911 which he did. He stayed with me while we waited.

As I was kneeling there, I realized what hoodie I was wearing. It was my half marathon hoodie from Montana that I had fairly recently completed. But I had just completed the Chicago Marathon in Oct 2017, so that hoodie was the most important. I knew that if I had been wearing the Chicago hoodie I would have seriously considered going back upstairs to change. Why? Because I knew it would get cut off by the ambulance crews and then thrown away at the hospital. I would never see that hoodie again. Now would I have actually gone back upstairs to change clothes with bullets in my head and blood running out of my head? Hehe I can't answer that. I do know that I would have seriously considered it. Of course, there was the neighbor too that could have helped, but you never know about me.

After that crazy thought, I was kneeling there going over and over in my head what else I needed to do or if there was something else I could do to help my situation. I kept thinking. Suddenly, a wave of calmness and peace came over me as if God was saying "It's okay. You did your part. I have it from here." I knew I had done everything I could do and it was time to let the crews do their jobs. Or to shut up, and not to tell the medics how to do their jobs.

Lucky for them, I don't remember that part. The last thing I remember is kneeling on the sidewalk with a police officer standing next to me. He was on his radio. They were trying to figure out how they were going to get me to the ambulance because it was still an active shooter scene. They hadn't found Mick yet and wouldn't for two hours. I was told I was talking and answering questions in the ambulance, but I have absolutely no recollection of that.

On the way to the hospital, I started having seizures, which is quite normal for head injury patients, especially severe trauma. The next thing I remember is fighting on the ET intubation tube. I remember several times being semi-conscious and knowing that tube was in my throat. That is such a horrible feeling especially when you don't know what is going on.

In time, I was taken off of the ventilator. I don't remember a whole lot and some blanks will be filled in later. I was told my sister was on her way flying. My parents kept calling from Montana, but still hadn't left to make the trip. A couple of my supervisors came to visit me soon after the ET tube was pulled. As soon as I saw them, I told them that I wouldn't be able to make my next shift. They laughed.

I was able to talk to my sister on the phone on her layover. She asked me how I was feeling to which I replied, "Like I got hit by a Mack truck {long pause} or got shot in the head." She said she knew then that I'd be okay because I still had my sense of humor. I was then told that my parents would not be coming. What! What kind of parents don't show up when their daughter is dying? What parents decide that their own comfort is more important than when their daughter is fighting for her life? Say what? Yes, my parents refused to come to come to the hospital while I was dying.

Be there!

Will you be there for me when I need a hand?

Will you be there for me when I fall?

Will you be there for me in my darkest hour?

You say "Yes!"

But do you mean it?

Will you be there for me at my worst?

Will you be there for me when my health is failing?

Will you be there for me when I'm sad?

You say, "I will be there".

But do you seriously mean it?

Will you be there when I'm angry?

Will you be there when I seem unlovable?

Will you be there when I am on my deathbed?

Will you be there if no one else is?

You say, "I will never leave you".

Do you truly understand those words you say?

Yes! Yes! Yes! I may not know exactly the situation I am getting into, BUT I will always be there.

 I will love you at your best and love you at your worst and all the in between.

I will love you now and still when you are gone.

"Why?" you ask thinking you don't deserve this.

Because you are a true friend.

Because you love me for who and what I am with no judgment.

Because you have taught me how to love, how to give, and how to live.

I must stand by my "Go big or go home" philosophy.

If something is worth doing....

When something is worth living for...

When someone is worth loving...

If something is worth fighting for...

By all means, do it!

Give it your all!

-BonniferWW

Chapter 2

The Parents

Let it go!

When you discover the truth about someone...

When you find that someone close to you wasn't who they claimed...

When your heart severely hurts with emotional pain...

Let it go!

When those who claim to love you refuse to be by your side in troublesome times...

When they are full of excuses as to why they cannot be there...

When they are only after the drama and personal attention they think they will get from it

Let it go!

When the worst possible tragedy happens to you....and you survive...

When you wish you could have done more to help...

When your heart breaks for the whole situation...

Let it go!

When sleep is a rough fight every night...

When the nightmares trouble your soul...

When the mind's replays of the events are constant...

Let it go!

I cannot change the past.

I cannot change people's choices and decisions.

I cannot change the outcome.

BUT

I can…

Let it go!

-BonniferWW

How do you write about someone who raised you, but on the other hand didn't? Others had to "raise" you. How do you write about someone who claims they taught you life, but didn't? Others had to "teach" you. How do you write about someone who says they were the "perfect parent", but were far from it?

 Well, I don't know either, but I'm going to give it a go. Now first off, let me get this straight. I do love my parents. I completely do. I love them for bringing me into this world. I love them for giving me my twin sister. I love them for getting me to my adult years. I love them for teaching me what they did. I love that they taught me to work hard. I love them for everything that they did for me. Now do I love and appreciate their methods? Nope! But we'll get to that point later on.

Dad grew up in a large family of 6 kids. I don't know much about his childhood because he rarely talked or mentioned it. I do know he was an all-star basketball player in high school. Even into his adult year, as in when I was in my young adult years, he was still upset at his parents for not attending his games. He stated a couple times of how his parents played favorites which very well could have been. Who knows? He was born to Andy and Retha Van Deraa in 1949 in Indiana.

Mom grew up in a small family of three, but really two. Her sister came along much later. Growing up, it was just her and her brother. She talked about her divorced mother having various boyfriends throughout the years and she would be in the kitchen cooking for them. Mom was born to Louise B. in 1953 in Cincinnati, Ohio. There were a few times that a pastor would preach against divorce in a church service. Then we'd get home. Mom would almost threaten us; it seemed like telling my sister and I to never ever get divorced. I remember feeling scared and very confused. Why would I get divorced? I didn't even have a boyfriend.

I understand they both came from imperfect backgrounds, but then who does right? They always told me "We want better for you than what we had". I get that, but why would you go to the extreme of the extreme? In the following pages, I am going to attempt to explain their philosophies as I remember it, as I saw them, and as I felt them internally.

Mom and Dad married and four years later my sister and I arrived. Mom said that they didn't know that she was having twins until she was fixing to deliver. Her doctor was constantly on her case for gaining too much weight, but she was strictly following the eating plan. Mom never talked about our birth. We asked, but she would get super mad. Yoana and I have always felt like we had, or should have had, or have been missing a brother. Whenever we have mentioned this to Mom, she would get seriously pissed off. And I do mean pissed off. We've never told anyone this before, at least I haven't, but we wonder if we were really triplets. What if we were and Mom and Dad, for whatever reason - personal or medical, decided to kill him off? That would surely have made her royally mad when we had figured it out. But it's all speculation and something we will probably never know. There was a time once when Mom thought she might be pregnant and had told us. We were in junior high. We were so excited at the thought of having a baby brother or sister. We were hoping Mom would come home from the doctor with it confirmed that she was pregnant. Again, Mom was not at all happy with us that we were so excited. Maybe not tell us at all then? She ended up not being pregnant either by the way.

Mom and Dad went to church every week. In fact, it was twice on Sunday and then Wednesday night too. They were and still are independent fundamental bible believing Baptist. By golly. So, as you can imagine, I grew up very conservative. But then on top of that, Mom and Dad had their own set of rules. But we'll get to that in the next chapter. They believed in the Trinity - God the Father, God the Son, and God the Holy Spirit. They believe the virgin Mary gave birth to Jesus and that Jesus was crucified to pay for the sins of the world. Eventually, all humans will be ordered to stand before God to be judged for what type of life they chose to live here on earth.

Of course, there is so much more to it than that and this book is not about religion or theology.

There was no deviation from the regular church schedule. It didn't matter if we went on vacation or to Grandma's house. There was always church on those days. When I was sick, I even felt guilty for staying home. It may have been the flu or period cramps or whatever else with a fever. I felt guilty. To be honest though, as I got older, I didn't mind the break from going when I was sick. It was almost like a breather from everything being crammed down my throat. Now, don't get me wrong. I believe in God and I did then too. But when you're constantly having it shoved down without anytime to process a single thing or to figure out what you personally believe or not, a tiny break is a gift - even when sick. I will admit that when I was older, but still living at home, there were a few times, I faked being sick because I just couldn't go. I couldn't do all the hypocrisy nonsense. Plus, I needed that breather again.

I remember at a young age being allowed to play often and somewhat freely. I remember Mom even being more involved with my childhood antics. But I still can never remember a time when she truly got involved like a Mom would. I picture a Mom getting involved such as tea parties and trips to the zoo or outings to the park. Dad rarely did and usually that was when he and I would go to a minor league baseball team or he'd play volleyball with us in the backyard.

The older we grew, the more "responsibilities" we had and the less free time we would see. By responsibilities, I mean that for whatever reason, Mom and Dad felt the need to make the kids have full responsibility for literally most of the chores (including cooking meals), while they sat and watched tv. Mom did sit at her desk, pay bills, and write letters, but that was the extent.

Now, let me explain this a bit deeper. Mom kept a list of chores that my sister and I would have to complete before we were allowed to do anything for ourselves or anything fun. Sounds decent right? Well, this list included everything from basic weekly chores to wiping down the baseboards to odd chores she'd write down to deep cleaning the kitchen. When she happened to cook supper, but made a mess on the stove, my sister and I had to clean it up.....even her burnt messes. When we thought the list was done, she'd check things over. If there was anything wrong, which there always was, her response was "you didn't dust the ....." or "you didn't wash the .....". Even if we had dusted or washed whatever it was, if it had a spot on it because it had been a day or two since dusted, it became a "you didn't do this" thing. So needless to say, we rarely ever even tried to get the dreaded list done. Ever! Why try when it won't ever be done right anyhow.

Now again, please keep in mind, I love my parents. I don't know what they were thinking then or even now today to make them even consider their methods of raising their children the way they chose to. Sometimes I wish I could go back in time knowing what I know now but be back then with this knowledge. Know what I mean Vern? How that would have rocked their world.

Mom and Dad believed in spanking. They spanked for everything. There was no grounding or time outs or counting to 3 or anything else. Spanking was it. If you looked at them with a look that they thought was with attitude, you risked getting a spanking. If you stood up for yourself, you risked getting punished for being "defensive". If you got in an argument with your sister, you could get spanked. If you forgot homework at school, you could get spanked. If you got an F on a test, you'd get spanked. If Dad was quizzing you for a test the next day and you gave a wrong answer to a question, you also got spanked. No joke! Those are just a few examples.

Now these spankings weren't just a few swats either. There were many swats. There were several times that I tried to count how many swats I was getting. I'd lose count around 12-15 swats and still they kept going. It was as if they had to burn off their anger or bitterness over something else through hurting me before they could stop. It was to the point of leaving bruises on my butt. I told Mom once about her leaving bruises when we were younger. Her response was, "well you never complained about bruises back then". Of course not! Back then, I thought I deserved them. So many times, I even thought I was adopted because of the way I was treated. So many times I cried myself to sleep praying that someone at school or church would ask or do something to make home life better. But nothing happened.

Were there happy times? Yes, of course there were. I think the younger I was, the happier times were. Why? Because I didn't know any different. Because I was more oblivious to the world around me. I was far less worried about the adult life I would have to eventually grow up to. I didn't have to be concerned yet about adult worries. So, trips to Granny's house were okay. Otherwise, that's a whole another chapter of its own.

Things really began becoming difficult when I tried to begin to fly. You know when kids start to become teenagers, start to want to be treated like adults, and then eventually expect to have adult responsibilities? Yeah, all of that. Well, that didn't go so well in this household. Every time my sister and I would attempt to fly, be it something little or big, Mom and Dad would blow their top and then there would be a blow up. Here's an example of something big. I was still living at home and had been trying to do things on my own to not be so dependent on my parents. One morning, I headed out to the alley where my mini van was parked to go run some errands. I had a flat tire. I called Dad all worried that now I was going to have to replace a tire. He calmly told me where the tire pump was in the garage and to not worry about the tire. There would be no need to replace it. I went inside to tell Mom that I hadn't left yet when she informed me that Dad had purposely let air out of the tire because I wasn't being dependent enough on them. Oh, how I was mad! How do you do that to your child? Why would you do that? Are you not supposed to raise your children to leave home, not be dependent upon you forever?

Love. How do you define love? How do you show your love? How do you live your love? It's an unconditional love right or you hope it to be. You love someone no matter what they do or don't do, even when you are mad at or disappointed in them. How do you live it? You live it by treating others the way you would like to be treated. You live it by treating everyone like you would treat your mother or grandmother (from a good home life). You live it by showing this love no matter what, no matter how you are feeling, no matter what kind of day you are having, and no matter how you are treated. That is unconditional love.

Mom and Dad? Nope! If one or the other was mad at me, they would refuse to say, "I love you". Mom would yell and throw temper tantrums. Dad would just do whatever Mom told him to as far as standing up to us. No backbone or fight to stand up to Mom. If it was a day something special was supposed to happen, such as Valentine's Day (Dad always gave us flowers and Mom always packed special lunches that day.), and we acted as though we were "expecting it", it was gone in a heartbeat. If I had so much as a thought of a bad attitude according to them, they would suddenly act as if they didn't love me.... you know the hold-me-off-at-arm's-length type of treatment. Extremely difficult for a child.

We moved around a lot growing up and it always seemed to be tied to Mom and Dad being asked to leave whatever particular church we were attending. Now of course, they never told it to us that way. As children, they also never told us the real story either. Even as grown adults, when they were asked to leave a church, they still didn't tell us the truth. We always went to a private Christian school. (We'll get into that more in the next chapter.) Mom and Dad were usually teachers there too until we were in high school. The first church I remember is when Yoana and I had just finished 2nd grade. The story we were told later on in life was that the church had voted to close the school and so they had to move on.

That summer, we drove a lot with Mom and Dad looking for teaching jobs. I remember driving up to Maine and Canada, but otherwise I forget. We then landed in Novi, Michigan for 1 year. Dad was the school principal. That school was miserable. I constantly heard "just because you're the principal's kid". We sure didn't get any special treatment, but had to earn everything just like everyone else. Well, sure enough, they were asked to leave there too. I never was told a decent reason for that one so I won't speculate except to say that it probably falls in with the rest of them.

That summer, we stayed with our grandparents for several weeks. It was our Dad's grandparents. Mom and dad traveled looking for jobs. Sometimes we went with, other times not. It was more fun to stay at Grandma and Grandpa's house seriously. Cousins were there. More freedom to play. Huge yard to play. It was great.

They eventually found jobs in Mattawan Michigan at a school. Dad would teach History, English, Geography type classes and Mom would teach music classes. We managed to stay here for 4 years before they were asked to move on. They had begun causing ruckus in the church and asked to not come back. Yoana and I weren't told what really happened there either.

By this time, I was wondering if it was even possible to stay in one place for more than 3 or 4 years. Friends and various family members had stayed in the same place for their whole lives, but here we were moving it seemed like every other year.

In the summer before 8th grade, we moved to South Bend, Indiana. I only hoped this spot would be different. Again, we started at a new Christian school. But this time, Mom and Dad weren't teaching here. Scary? Yes! A relief? Possibly.

The first couple of years went well, but then Mom and Dad were back to causing trouble again slowly but surely. Some of the teachers would take it out on Yoana and I. One teacher would purposely walk on the other side of the hallway when he saw us coming. He was my history teacher so no way to absolutely avoid him. Another incident was with the science teacher. He accused us of cheating because he had issues with our parents. Literally our whole class laughed at him in class when he said that. Yes, he accused us in front of the whole class by the way. That did come back to bite him in the ass later.

How do you claim to love someone who you never allow to "breathe"? How do you say you care when you show no love? How do you say "I love you" when the next moment you turn around and spew anger?

That is not being a parent.

What is being a kid in this family?

Blood is NOT Thick Than Water

I should hate you for what you've done,

For it is absolutely deplorable.

I should despise you for what I am to you,

For it is incredibly difficult.

I should loathe you for your treatment of me,

For it is very horrifying.

I should detest you for your lack of concern in my darkest hours,

For it is horribly disturbing and disgusting.

It makes me feel the need to vomit.

It gives me the urge to cry.

It makes me feel angry.

It gives me the urge to punch a pillow.

You have never truly cared about me.

You have never truly loved me.

You have never truly been there for me.

You have never truly held my hand through the storm.

Where was the unconditional love?

Where was the example of two people truly in love?

Where was the rock that parents are supposed to be?

Where was the parent's strength a child can lean on?

Nowhere to be found.

Not here. Not there.

It is not anywhere.

For it never did exist.

You found the time to attend an aunt's funeral.

You found the funds to attend an extended family member's goodbye.

You found the flight ticket to attend a special person's celebration of life.

But you ignored your daughter in her own darkest hour.

The darkest hour which she was supposed to not survive.

The darkest hour when she needed your strength.

The darkest hour when it could have been her last.

The darkest hour when being a parent should have mattered the most.

How can you live with yourself?

How can you not care about your own kid?

How can you not hate yourself?

How can you even fake your happiness?

I feel sorry for you, I truly do.

I have been horribly hurt by you. I truly am.

I have been seriously abused by you. I truly have.

I have lost all respect I ever had towards you. I'm truly empty.

I have nothing else to say.

I have nothing else to give.

I have nothing else to offer.

I have nothing else to ask.

If you want me, want me in the good as well as the bad.

If you need me, need me in the good as well as the bad.

If you love me, love me in the good as well as the bad.

If you care for me, care in the good as well as the bad.

-BonniferWW

Chapter 3

My Childhood

Life!

Sometimes life is good, but right now it's hard.

Sometimes life is fun, but right now it's not.

Sometimes life is joyful, but right now it's depressing.

Sometimes life's a breeze, but right now it's a 200 m.p.h. Wind storm.

Sometimes life is easy, but right now it's extremely difficult.

Sometimes life is smooth, but right now it's rough.

Sometimes life is fulfilling, but right now it's emptying everything I've got.

Sometimes life is the greatest thing ever, but right now, it's the most horrid thing I've ever been through.

Sometimes life is meaningful, but right now it's full of questions.

Sometimes life is empowering, but right now it's full of denial.

Sometimes life is strengthening, but right now it's weakening me to my knees.

Sometimes the worst times turn into the best of times.

Sometimes the worst times turn into a life purpose.

Sometimes the worst times turn into times of showing strength.

Sometimes the worst times turn into finding answers.

Sometimes the worst times turn into beauty.

Sometimes the worst times turn out to be extremely valuable.

Sometimes the worst times turn into proving others wrong.

Sometimes the worst times turn into a rainbow.

Sometimes the worst times bring the brightest sky.

Sometimes the worst times bring about the greatest and best life you ever dreamed possible.

Don't ever give up! Don't ever give in! But give it all you've got! Stand up! Be proud! For you've just kicked life in the booty.

After reading the last chapter, I'm sure you have a little bit of an idea of what's coming. Please just hang on and please do not make any assumptions. Please just read what is written. This is extremely difficult to write just as it is probably to read.

Now again, I love my parents, but I do not love their methods, their beliefs, their thinking, or what they did to me and my sister. I have serious issues with that. Huge issues. What follows is nothing that I haven't already said to them in person and in writing. They know how I feel and think about things. Their response, by the way, was pure laughter. So I feel absolutely no hindrance in writing what needs to be said or in what flows out during this story. My goal is NOT to tattle or wave a flag shouting "look how horrible my childhood was". Far from it for I'd seriously rather not think of it ever again. But my purpose in all of this is to be able to encourage someone or maybe even a few people. If it does that, then my struggles and agonies of writing this become completely worthwhile. My pain of going through it as a child became easier to bear because I was able to help someone.

My twin sister, Yoana, and I were born in Ypsilanti Michigan in 1977. We were born prematurely, common for twins, and were jaundiced too. So we had to spend some time in the NICU. We were to be the only two children born to our parents. We moved around a lot which of course didn't help us in a lot of ways growing up. Mom and Dad insisted we went to a private Christian school from kindergarten through our senior year of high school. Many times I had wished I were in a public school for the many more opportunities for one. But many times throughout my childhood, I had wished there had been someone at school I felt like I could talk to. There wasn't, but I had the thought there would have been more options for that at a public school too. Plus more people to notice the odd situation my sister and I were growing up in. So many more options in a public school for education, sports, after school activities, etc. "Oh but they teach sex education and don't teach the bible". Really? "I don't want my child exposed to the world and the devil's work." Uh, did you know that your child lives in the world and is already exposed to the "devil's work"? These weren't the exact words out of Mom and Dad's mouth as for the reasons for not putting us in public school, but it's a start. I'd rather know what sex was at a young age than to grow up only having a vague idea, and then having to do an internet search to figure out the rest. Yes, that was me. More on that in a second because otherwise I'm going to be getting ahead of myself here. The bible should be taught at home if it's that important.

If you desire to be affiliated with a particular religion, then so be it. My personal belief is that it isn't about religion because religion is a man made up mess. Instead, it is about a personal relationship with God as in conversation back and forth like I would with a close friend. So to say that you have to live completely separated from the world, as in your kids go to a private Christian school and have no social lives, gives them utterly no reason at all to even try to want to live differently, or to be leaders, or to be separate from the world, or to be a different crowd. It's however you want to look at it there. But when you aren't allowed to do anything, be around anyone, or talk to anybody not associated with your very tiny approval by the parents crowd, it's almost like what's the point of trying. Not sure if this is making sense. But when you're kept so extremely sheltered and so extremely under control, it makes you just want to go out and rebel. It wouldn't really be rebelling because it would actually be doing what's right but would just be rebelling according to Mom and Dad. Then there's the issue of when you become an adult. Because of being so sheltered and being kept so naive and such, you have no clue how to act in the outside world. You have no clue how to do anything in the outside world. You have no clue about such things as words having double meaning, how guys think differently from women, or so much more.

Yes, I didn't know what sex was until later in school. I will not disclose at exactly what age because it's embarrassing. I had a very good idea of how it was done previously, but it was never confirmed by either a knowledgeable adult, a book, the internet, etc. until later. Yoana and I would talk and verify our thoughts concerning the matter, which we were both on the same page about. Did we ask Mom? Well, we tried. That preteen age when girls start to have questions about that sort of thing. Here's the thing.......it didn't matter if it was sex or boys or a new swear word we'd never heard, or a new Disney movie, or anything. If we asked Mom something, it was basically a guaranteed interrogation session. Who did you hear that from? Why do you want to know? How did you hear that? Who put that idea into your head? Uh maybe it's a ten-year-old girl asking a question because she's ten years old and that's what ten-year-old girls do. It is that age. But she was that way about everything. So we quickly stopped asking her anything. If we were worried about something such as puberty changes, we asked each other if she was experiencing it also.

We weren't allowed to wear pants or shorts even in the dead of winter or the heat of summer. Nope. We had to wear culottes and long skirts. In the winter, we could wear sweats under our skirts if it were really cold, but you know how fashionable that looks. We were asked often if we were Pentecostal because of our long skirts or long and full culottes that looked like skirts.

We weren't allowed to go to friend's houses if they had older brothers or teenage brothers because of "things they might do" and "and teenage hormones". Do you know how embarrassing that is to tell a close friend why you can't come over to their house? Horrible! We weren't allowed to go to the movie theater because "bad things happen in the dark at the movies". I asked Mom and Dad once why we couldn't go to a G-rated movie. They always despised smoking and alcohol so I used that against them so to speak. I asked them, "So if you can't go to the movies to see a G rated movie because that money might go to support a R rated movie, then what about the grocery store? You despise smoking and drinking. You go to the grocery store to buy veggies, ice cream, and bread, but what if some of that money goes to purchase alcohol and cigarettes for the grocery store? Oh how the parents did not like that question. In fact, they became quite mad and had no answer.

I can count on one hand the number of times we were actually allowed to go play outside with the neighbor kids. Mom's response was always, "No! Your list isn't done." That list was never done. You're only a kid once. You only get to play during one stage in your life. Nothing was ever done right or good enough. Whether it was that list, or schoolwork or the dishes, or setting the table or us cooking supper. Mom always found something that she didn't like. Too dusty, water spots, you didn't try hard enough, too spicy, too dull. So many excuses. She even claimed that a B- wasn't really even a B. I asked her once if a B- isn't a B, then what is it because it sure isn't a C? Again, no answer.

We had to ask permission for almost everything…..literally. From getting something to eat to doing laundry to going outside to play with the dog to getting a drink of water. Yes, a drink of water. When Mom and Dad told us to do something, you had better immediately jump. Then while jumping, you can ask how high to jump, but only after beginning to jump. Otherwise, you bet you'd get spanked and most likely, a hard and long spanking. There were no short respectable spankings. They knew no meaning of respecting the other party, aka the child. They literally thought that was a laughable idea.

How do you be a kid in this environment? How do you learn what is expected when no one really knows because it changes on the mood? How do you be a child in a world where you're expected to already be grown up? You can't. You only dream about being a kid. I'd see other kids playing in yards, riding bicycles, or talking about a vacation they were going to take with their family, and I only wished it was me.

But it wasn't. I had a bicycle until I outgrew it. We didn't go on vacations. We went to Grandpa and Grandma V's house or Granny's house. Anything else was while they were job hunting for teaching jobs or something like that.

Or lied so they could win a contest with a hotel stay gift certificate prize. Yep! At the time, we were going to Grace Baptist Church. Now I think it's Granger Christian. They put on a contest for all attendees to have family devotions. They had prizes through the several weeks of the contest. To qualify for the grand prize with the hotel package, you had to have family devotions at least like 4 or 5 times a week. There were weeks when we never had them. When we did have them, it was a joke to me because it wasn't real. There was one purpose and one purpose only why they were having them and that was to win that contest. Nothing else mattered. If it had been real, then it would have been more frequent. It wouldn't have been lied about. It also would have been continued after the contest was over. So yes, in case you're wondering, they "won" the contest, but they lied to do it. In actuality, we never even came close to winning that contest and sure didn't deserve it.

To this day, I do not understand how you can have children, but then purposely mess them up for the rest of their lives. Mom and Dad both came from childhoods with great education. Dad had a great family at least in part. Mom had at least one loving parent. They both had freedom to explore and do their thing. So I don't understand why would you suddenly turn to the ugly extreme? Rumor is that Dad was a completely different person before Mom came along.....life of the party, laughter, hilarious, jokester, etc. But as soon as he said, "I do", things began to change.

Many many many times, Yoana and I came home from school in tears because of being mistreated, made fun of, and bullied. We cried on Mom's shoulder. She'd listen and tell us it would be okay. But then that would be it until the next day. Repeat. Never once did she tell us what to say to the bullies or even encourage me to stand up for myself. Never. Do you enjoy seeing your children suffering? You want your children to not be "in the world", but you aren't even teaching them how to stand on their feet in a supposed "Christian" environment.

I don't get this. I seriously don't. I was about 18 or 19, when I told Mom that I was never going to have any children. I was dead serious, and it had been after one of her mean episodes. I was over it and wasn't saying this out of anger or frustration. When Mom heard that, she busted out laughing and said she didn't believe me and that I would change my mind. Well, here it is many years later. I'm 43 years old at the time of writing this and I still have no children. It's a firm promise Mother. She has still never once asked me why I would say such a thing. Many times, in dealing with us, they never asked why. They just acted in their anger or emotions of whatever they were at that moment. Anyhow, I chose to never have children because I didn't want my parents to have access to any more children to mess up and ruin. I didn't want the drama and lies either. Even at that young age when I told Mom that, I knew then how evil their character was.

We were spanked a lot yes as we talked about earlier, but Mom and Dad also liked to withhold food. Such as making us sit at the dinner table with only a glass of water to watch everyone else eat while we got nothing else. Many times we didn't get supper and went to bed hungry. A few times, Mom would give us the option of being spanked or no supper. I'd pick no supper, but she'd spank me anyway.

Mom and Dad, but especially Dad only told me I was beautiful when I dressed how they wanted or fixed my hair how they wanted it fixed. If I tried something new with my hair, Dad's usual response was "Are you going to do something with your hair today?" Dad would also tell me I was fat and that guys don't like fat girls. Now mind you, this was junior high and high school. I was 5'6" - 5'10" and 170 pounds max here. I was in 7th grade when I broke 100 pounds. I thought I was fat, the scale would break, and the world was going to end, but I sure couldn't tell anyone that. How can I be fat when I'm at my height and perfect weight for my height? I didn't look fat. Only reason I looked awful was because of the horrendous clothes I wore. May as well have worn a head to toe potato sack. It would have had more shape to it then what I ever wore. Apparently, if anything showed skin or your body shape, it was a sin. Not sure where that's in the bible either. You can dress beautifully without being a tramp.

I don't understand why. Not sure if I do want to understand, but I do wish I could know the honest answer of why they chose to do this. I think I just said no and then yes to myself in back to back sentences. Ha-ha! It was a rough childhood and I'm so very glad it's over with. In the moment, there were so many times when I thought I couldn't take much more. I was even sure I was adopted because of the way Mom was.

Mom and Dad would tell me "I love you" only when they weren't mad. Otherwise, they refused to say it.

Speaking of "I love you", Dad and I had this game of sorts. Dad would say "I love you" in a goofy way and I would chase him around the house until he said it correctly. Well, the last time I played along he crossed the line in a big way. He pinned me against the wall. I somehow slid down to the floor where I was still pinned down. By this time, I was in tears and told him many times to stop tickling me and get off. It took several times of telling him before he did. I spent the rest of the day in my room in occasional tears. I never ever again played along. He tried several times to get me to, but when he said "I love you" in the goofy manner, I just stood there and stared at him. He eventually got the hint I wasn't playing. He never apologized for what he did and never even asked why I was no longer playing along.

I've talked to them many times. I've written letters to them. I've talked to pastors for help. One pastor was at a church that we all went to at the time. His response was "I'll talk to your parents." He never gave Yoana and I any advice at all. We were in our 20's at this point. His advice to the parents was to write up a contract that we'd have to sign if we wanted to stay living at home. Okay great! Well, there were 2 things on there that were huge NO's for us. 1) If you make a mess, you clean it up. Sounds good, but Mom never did it. If she made a mess in the kitchen, we had to clean up her mess. So no. 2) We'd have to stay living at home until we got married. Yes, you read that correctly. Now they had never raised us with that concept. This was the first time they had mentioned it. We basically burst with laughter and rolling of the eyes.

Mom and Dad told us we had 30 days to think about it. We told them we needed about 30 seconds if that. I told them I would NOT be signing the contract. Obviously, that is when my sister and I planned to move out.

How did my parents react to us telling them we were moving out? How did they react on moving day? How did they handle it afterwards and throughout time? Time will tell.

Fly. Rise. Breathe.

Someday I will fly.

Meanwhile you try to pull me down

Telling me I will never amount to much.

But you are wrong.

For I shall one day fly.

Someday I will rise

Meanwhile you try to bury me

In your lies and deceitful ways.

But you are wrong.

For I shall one day rise.

Someday I will breathe

Meanwhile you try to suffocate me

In your evil world and dark mind.

But you are wrong.

For I shall one day breathe.

Just one more step.

Just one more hour.

Just one more day.

Just another teardrop.

Just another drop of sweat.

Just another sweaty workday.

Then there in the distance.

Just a ways off.

Is that day.

That day I shall fly.

That day I will rise.

That day I will breathe.

It will be the day you will have failed.

It will be your day of shame.

It will be that day of fate you were warned about by many.

You thought you could make yourself look acceptable to others.

You thought you could fool those outside your house.

You thought you could keep your children under your control forever.

But then…

I flew.

I arose.

I breathed.

-BonniferWW

Chapter 4

Adventures of Being a Twin

When.......

When the burden seems too heavy....... help someone else carry their struggles.

When it seems you can't take another step.....help someone else take two.

When it seems the grief is too much.....make someone else smile.

When the pain seems to be too great.....find strength in those who have chosen to be by your side.

When the darkness is at its darkest.....let a friend be your light.

When you feel lost far beyond ever being found.....take that outstretched hand.

For in your darkest hour, you may still be someone else's brightest light.

In your darkest moment, you may give someone else strength to carry on.

Your smile,

Your grace,

Your strength,

Your determination,

Your tenacity,

Your heart.

It is in your darkest of dark moments

Where you see yourself for who you truly are,

Where you find what you are truly made of, and

Where you discover what you truly desire.

-BonniferWW

Have you ever met an identical twin? Have you ever been
able to have the privilege of getting to know a set of twins and
watching their unique relationship? What did you think of it?
Was it inspiring? Was it boring? Exciting? Interesting?

It isn't just anyone that can say they are a twin and it just anyone of those who can say they are an identical twin. Then no one else is me and my twin and never will you ever. Just in case you were wondering, I thought I'd help you out there. But in all seriousness (do we have to be serious?) being a twin is quite something special. Someone that is right there with you through life, understands you like nobody else can, can feel you emotionally when no one gets you, an automatic best friend, and the list goes on. This is far more than best friends or couples who have been married for decades or siblings who have close relationships. This is also far different. Now this is not a scientific book and no need to delve into that side of things here, but you get the idea.

Being a twin is full of fun and mischief and we sure did our share of it. Let me share some of it with you. When my sister and I were little, my mom would dress us in similar outfits so that others would be able to tell us apart. I was usually in blue and my sister was usually in pink. Plus my parents marked the bottom of our shoes.....mine with a B for Bonnie and my sister's with a Y for Yoana. Creative huh?

When we got older, we would dress alike, sometimes of our own accord. Sometimes we would dress completely differently. Sometimes we would dress alike completely by accident as in we would plan on dressing completely differently but would come out of our different bedrooms completely dressed alike. How does that happen? It's the twin thing.

Many times we'd play tricks on people, though sometimes playing tricks on people happened without us trying. We'll come back to that part though. As kids in elementary school, it was mostly changing clothes at school to fool our teachers. Looking back now, I see how gross that is to put on someone else's clothes in the middle of the day, but that was then as a child. You may not think anything of it, but ewwww.

As we grew older, the tricks became better. We both have worn glasses since we were around 18 months old. There was approximately a year in junior high where Yoana didn't have to wear glasses. We got home from the eye doctor. Dad was upstairs and Yoana went up there. Dad looked at her and thought she was me. He began chewing her out for her messy bedroom. She let him go on for a bit before she told him that she wasn't me. Oh we laughed about that one for a while. He did too.

We had a chemistry teacher in high school that was also a twin, but he was fraternal with a sister. We had assigned seats in his class. In his class, we would switch seats every once in a while. One day, he told us that if we did it again, he'd make us get up in front of the class and sing the national anthem. We were so shy back then that we never switched again in his class. Later on in the semester, he also accused us of cheating on Chemistry homework. We had to help each other because he stated in class that he was too busy to help students with Chemistry outside of class. He later apologized, but only after much drama. Dad had gone to talk to the principal. Mom majorly chewed us out at home "just in case it was really true". But our classmates stood by our sides because they knew it wasn't true. They flat out laughed when the teacher accused us in front of the class that day. But oh well.

Then there was our beloved English teacher, and yes we did really love him even though we despised English class. Oh and Literature class too. We'd have pop quizzes and many times, Yoana and I would get the same exact grade. We knew because we'd have to read our grade off in class to our teacher. Mr. Redmond would give us that look that said he thought it was "funny, interesting, and a good thing he trusted us" all in one. But he taught us so much and was very patient.

When Yoana was in paramedic school, I went to class for her one night for an hour. Yep, sure did! She always sat in the front row next to Tammy which is exactly what I did. Her class had a break about every hour or so. Things went off without a hitch. When we switched back, Tony asked Yoana what her sister was doing there. Me. She told him that we had switched on him during the last hour of class. He didn't believe her at first but was eventually convinced. He never did live that down.

So back to playing tricks on people without trying.....We had moved out on our own and were sharing an apartment. It was this time plus after Yoana moved out from that apartment up to Dowagiac MI. But one of us would be out in public and would see someone that knew the other sister. That person thought they knew whichever twin they saw when in reality they didn't, but they knew the other. I hope that makes sense. If they saw me, they really knew Yoana, but thought I was Yoana. I hope that helps. Well we'd let them carry on and on to the point that most of the time, they never found out that they were speaking to the opposite twin. Then whichever one of us that it happened to would call up the other one to tell her and we'd have an extreme giggle moment over it.

Being a twin isn't all sunshine and roses though. Sometimes it's ugliness and stormy. At the time of this writing, it is currently one of those times in mine and my twin's life. Things are a bit rocky. With my traumatic brain injury, I handle things differently than I once did. Yoana is still learning that. She has yet to realize that who I once was died January 23rd, 2018. I'm a different Bonnie now. But you know what, we'll get through this. We love each other far too much to let this go on for forever.

I'm sure you've heard stories of twins having strange symptoms when separated. Such as one is pregnant and goes into labor, and the other twin also has labor pains. Or one has a heart attack and the other has severe chest pain too.

Well, we've had some of these instances. I was still in Indiana and had a day off of work for once. All of a sudden, I had a gut feeling I had to call Yoana. I didn't have a clue why, but just had to call her immediately. She had been in Illinois visiting a friend and I was afraid that something had happened. I called and her friend answered which of course, scared me even more. Her friend said that Yoana was okay but was being loaded into the ambulance. She had been reaching into the passenger seat for something, wasn't paying attention, and had rolled her car. I was a mess until I was able to talk to her when she was able to talk at the hospital.

Then I was out here in Oklahoma by this time. I was at work running a call when I had a bad gut feeling that I had to call my sister. Crap! I had a patient and had to take care of that before I could call. I did and finished the call first. As soon as I could, I called. Yoana answered. She was emotional, teary, and a mess. She said that she had just been rear-ended by a semi but was again okay. Her car wasn't though.

Then on January 23, 2018, Yoana had a horrible headache that she couldn't get rid of. Tylenol, Ibuprofen, Caffeine, etc. Nothing would help it. Nothing would even take the edge off. Then she got the phone call about the shooting and that I had been shot. Now she knew why.

The good and the bad of being a twin.

Chapter 5

College Life

Smile!

What is in a smile?

Is it joy? Is it happiness? Is it a celebration?

What is in a smile?

Is it the truth or is it covering the truth?

Is a smile real or is it covering real pain?

What is in a smile?

Is it sadness? Is it depression? Is it darkness?

What is in a smile?

Sometimes forgetting my own trials to help someone else.

Sometimes forgetting my own trials because I'm scared.

Sometimes forgetting my own trials because I don't know how to deal with my struggles and I'm waiting.

Waiting for answers.

Waiting for time.

Waiting for strength.

Waiting for the sun to shine.

A smile is not always a smile of happiness.

Sometimes it's waiting.

Sometimes It's hiding.

Sometimes it's being carried on the strength of others.

Can you read beyond the top layer of that smile?

Sometimes it hides the bumps and scars of life.

Other times, it shows the happiness of life.

Sometimes it hides the sadness and struggles.

Other times, it shows the strength and confidence of battles won.

Sometimes a smile is truly a smile of pure joy.

Sometimes it's how I find the strength to take another step by making someone else smile that smile of joy.

-BonniferWW

Not everyone attends college. College isn't for everyone. Typically, a student will choose a few to several colleges they hope to attend based on what they have chosen to major in. Then apply to the schools to see which one they are accepted to. If able to, there may even be a visit to a few schools to see what campus life and classes are like. The student, at times with help from the parents, will then decide which college to attend.

That is not, however, how my parents saw things. My parents were determined that I was going to go to college, but it was going to be one college in particular. Northland Baptist Bible College. It didn't matter what I wanted to major in or be when I grew up or wanted to do with my life. That was where I was going to college. I'm not sure why you would do things that way, except that they were my parents. I can only look at their history.

Now, this college only had majors for those who wanted to be pastors, missionaries, or teachers. That was it! This college was also unaccredited. At first, they claimed they were accredited, but under a different type of accreditation.... like under "Christian schools" or something. But when I checked on it later after graduation (of course! Silly me!), it's never been accredited. That type of accreditation doesn't even exist.

So I went to work on this degree. I had decided to major in Home Economics because it was something I could use no matter what I ended up doing in life. Of course it was considered the "MRS degree", but whatever. I didn't care. I was taking it for me. Being in this type of atmosphere, I was also basically majoring in Bible. That was the difficult part. Some of it was interesting, but other classes were just boring. The theological classes were boring.

Spring semester of my Sophomore year, I needed another elective. So I took a First Responder course mostly because I wanted to know what to do in the case of an emergency. Up to this point, I had had no clue what to do. I would have stood there like a blubbering idiot while someone was lying on the ground gushing blood with a knife sticking out of their abdomen. Okay okay, I probably would have called 911, but not before panicking and freaking out.

I fell in love with that class and everything it taught. It taught me assessment skills that helped me to put order to the call or the scene. But those assessment skills and order was something I could slowly start applying to my own life. I had no order or anything. I didn't know how. So while my trying looked like a daily tornado at first, it was a start. I didn't know I was even trying to do this back then. I only know now by looking back. I grew so much in that class and knew I wanted to do EMS for the rest of my life.

There was one thing keeping me from starting my full career in EMS right away though. Can you guess? [cough]. My parents. I was so scared to tell them. Very scared. Instead, I didn't. I knew it would be a world war three to say the least if I did. A year later when my sister took the course and then decided to drop out of college and keep going with her EMS career, it was world war three and I had to watch it all. It was awful. Originally, Dad had told us we only had to go to Bible college for one year. Now they were getting so bent out of shape. She'd been in college where they had wanted her to go for two and a half years. Far past the agreed amount of time. She managed to get out of not going back.

I kept going back to college semester after semester. Sure, after that semester of First Responder, I was ready to save the world. I even got a first aid kit that year for Christmas. It had more in it than what you bought in the store. I saw to that. (Imagine that.) If I saw an accident, I'd check to make sure the police or someone was there before I passed by. If I saw someone fall, I'd make sure they were okay and didn't need further help. If I saw them fall from a distance, I'd stay put and make sure they got up okay before I left the area. Now this is something I would have done anyhow for the most part I think, but I had extra reason and more responsibility to do so.

How did I make it past the last 2 years? One day of classes at time. Since the school believed that you shouldn't go into debt and they wanted their students to graduate debt free, it took me seven years to graduate with a four-year degree. Side note of humor is that that school went into debt expanding their campus, couldn't make the payments, and are no longer in business. Oh how that still brings me a chuckle. Anyhow, I was in my senior year when Mom and Dad suddenly decided that I had to call my Grandpa and ask him for money to pay my school bill so that I would be able to finish. Do you know how humiliating that is? How embarrassing. In my opinion, the parents should be taking care of the child. It isn't that the college age child is helpless obviously, but why would you throw that on the child out of the blue? Oh by the way, it was out of the blue they said your school bill won't be paid for so ask Grandpa. They would pull nonsense like that often and not just with college bills. But how are you supposed to plan life if you can't trust those who are supposed to be there for you? How are you supposed to learn to be an adult when time and time again, your parents fail you?

Well, I finished school in December of 2001, but had to wait until May of 2002 to officially graduate. Meanwhile, I worked at a small Mom and Pop magic shop. I ended up having to quit my job because of two reasons. The main reason was because the mold in the building was setting off my asthma. The second reason was because they refused to let me off work for my graduation. So one took care of the other. Now if I had to do it all over, I would have just dropped out of college after the First Responder course. But everything happens for a reason.

Am I upset that I went to college? Not at all. Am I disappointed in the way it was handled? Sure am. Did I have a good time at college? Sometimes. I made a few really good friends that I still have today. If this college were still in business today, would you recommend them? Why or why not? No I would not. Very close minded. Most of the instructors teach close minded also. In all of my years there, I had one instructor who went against the grain. He made you think and made you figure out what and why believed something, even if it went against what your parents and the school taught. It was okay to go against the grain and flow. Am I glad I went to this college? Yes sure I am. It taught me a lot of who my parents believe they are and helped me to understand them. I will never understand them though. It was the first place I began to learn to stand on my own two feet. There are so many memories in that place.... good and bad. It's where I began to learn to stand up to Mom and Dad, too. They chose to blame it on some other things, but in reality, it was college. If you don't want to lose control of your kids and if you don't want your kids to taste the tip of freedom, then never ever send them to college. NEVER! This of course applies to extremely sheltered homes at least. Others I do not know about, but I'm sure are very different.

So, yes, I'm very glad I went to college. I'm very glad it was that college. I learned a lot there.... including what I wanted to do with my life. That was the biggest thing. It was just a matter of time before I was able to begin my EMS dream.

Chapter 6

Growing into an Adult For Real

Scars

You have them and so do I.

Some are invisible and others are not.

Memories - good or bad

Experiences - horrible or epic

Scars are what life is made of.

We all do have them.

Some are painful and others are not.

Memories - hilarious or maddening

Experiences - educational or hell on earth

Scars are what life is made of.

Each individual has a few of these.

Some are tender while others are not.

Memories - tearful or laughter

Experiences - loved or despised

Scars are what life is made of.

Scars?

Emotional. Physical. Mental. And so much more.

Why must they hurt so?

Why must they bring such pain?

Why such reminders?

Why the loneliness and fear?

Why? To give you wings.

Why? To give you wings so that others may also fly.

Why? To help you grow strong and tall.

Why? To help you grow strong and tall so that others will be watered.

Why? To help you remember how truly strong, special, and tenacious you are.

Why? To help you remember that you are seriously oh so loved by oh so many.

Scars? Love them. Touch them. Feel them. Learn from them.
Share them. Celebrate them.

-BonniferWW

Do you really grow up into an adult? Do you really ever
reach

adulthood? Is there a time that you actually reach that adult

maturity? Or even just maturity? I'd take that alone too. Do
you

ever really stop growing into an adult? Do you ever stop
maturing

or/and growing as an adult? Do you have to stop growing
into an

adult? Is there ever a time that you reach when you think
"Okay,

I've arrived. I can go back home now."?

I hope there isn't because I love learning and I love exploring
this great big world we have as ours. I love to get up each and
every day and watch the world around me. I love to watch
people but then also watch what the critters are doing too.
You can learn something from everything and everyone
around you. From the bumblebee to the toddler to the
homeless guy to the mom with the young child to the clerk at
the hotel working in his retirement to the pesky mosquito.

A baby is born into this world knowing how to do absolutely nothing and must learn in time, how to do everything. Over time, that child will grow while learning constantly. Before long, that child is an adult. But is that adult prepared for adulthood? Did that child learn everything necessary for adulthood? Did the parents teach everything needed for life's journey? Will that child fail because adults failed him? Will that child become a product of his environment? Will that child grow in spite of his parents, his environment, etc. and become an adult to be reckoned with? Will this child grow to show other lost children how it's done, how to do it, and then be their guiding light? Only time and God knows.

I was once a very lost child, lost in the darkness. I'd probably never would have made it to actual adulthood except that many took me by the hand and led me. If I had been left to wander, I would have found myself still left at Mom and Dad's house at the age of 30, yes 30, and probably older too. I know 30 is a safe probable guess though. Remember what they said about me living at home until I was married off....... even if I was 30 or 40 or older. Can you imagine that? Me living with the parents at the ripe age of 47? Haha!

Me: I don't know if I can come over tonight. I have to ask my Mom.

Guy: Uh how old are you?

Me: I know but Mom says her house her rules.....even though I pay rent. Just a minute.

(Goes to ask Mom)

Me: Mom wants to know exactly where we are going to go? for how long? who we are going to be with? What church do you go to? Why you don't go to her church? How do you know you're a Christian? Who are your parents?

Guy: (interrupts) You're crazy! I'm gone.

Me: I'd be crazy if that paragraph was true as happened, but no.

I didn't know it then, but I was slowly being prepared for adulthood. Each little piece of happening was a bit of preparation for adulthood. Each adult separate from the parents that came into my life helped me reach that spot a little quicker. From schoolteachers to friend's parents to coworkers. It was even roommates in college or conversations had sitting in classes in college or watching the behaviors and consequences of others.

How do you knowingly let your child grow up like that, send him out into the world, and then one) expect the child to survive, but two) expect the world to raise your child? There I go off on that tangent again don't I? I didn't know what those poofy things are that you shower with until I was in college. I didn't know about shaving armpits until college either. I knew about shaving legs, but that was only because you had to shave your legs in order to wear "pantyhose" ......right?

I never learned how to do my nails from my mother. I learned it from watching many people over the years. My parents never pierced my ears. I went on my own and got my ears pierced on September 11th, 2001. I've had several emergency surgeries and not once were my parents there.

Mom could barely sew, but claims she taught us to sew. Teachers taught us to make basic clothing. Grandma taught me to make detailed clothing. Mrs. Janke (college instructor) taught me how to sew professionally. Grandma taught me her love for her quilts, her cooking, her sewing, and her love for Grandpa.

Janet became a friend and invited me to her church. She became like a big sister. She was there to ask questions to......even the dumb and embarrassing questions that you don't want to ask anyone except your sister. She began helping with the shyness and the public awkwardness. Connie at work helped to help me become a better and stronger EMT. (Volunteer EMT at the time.) Ashley, tech at the hospital, taught me how to be confident there.

I never learned things like confidence until my EMS career. "Fake it until you make it." Right? That goes for many things besides confidence. I know this isn't the chapter on EMS right now, but these chapters are going to overlap a bit. Maybe a lot at times.

Conversation is an art most never learn. It takes skill. I never learned to truly talk to people until my EMS career either. Sure I have a long list of questions I have to get through for an assessment, but in that process, there's all sorts of conversation included. From memories, to health related to the humorous. There are rabbit trails and sidetracks and so much more. I've learned so much about myself and about the person I'm talking to through conversation. There will be many more stories about conversation and such later on in this book.

 I wish things could have been different, but I also know that if they had been different, I sure wouldn't be here writing this book, now would I? There's always a reason something happens, the good/bad/ugly. What happened 5 years ago prepared me for today in some way. It also prepared me for tomorrow. Things I went through as a child helped to prepare me for the day that forever changed my life. Those few years of running.....each training run, each race, each rough workout with the trainer.....all worked together to prepare and ready me for Jan 23, 2018. I was in the best shape of my life then and the docs say that is a big reason I survived. Anyways, everything that happens prepares me for something down the road or can be used as preparation for down the road.....however you desire to look at it.

 While my mother didn't allow me to run in upper elementary age or she didn't teach me proper things or she thought abusive methods were acceptable ways of teaching, I made it through to the other side. I survived. I can help others who need the extra shove and pull to get through. I can help those who need the encouraging ear for whatever the reason is whether it be abuse or lack of tools or lack of strength. Whatever it is.

Chapter 7

Life as the Shy One

You are beautiful!

You are beautiful just the way you are!

No makeup.

Bed head.

Pajamas.

You are beautiful just as you are!

The tears.

The anger.

The scars.

You are beautiful just you as you!

The struggles.

The nightmares.

The flashbacks.

You are so beautiful just you for real!

No masks.

Nothing hidden.

No secrets.

You are very beautiful just all of you and not in part.

For if one little detail of you were not to be, then you would not be who you are.

For if the scars you carry did not exist, then you would not have your story to share.

For if your struggles were easy and fair, then you would not be the strong one that you are.

You are beautiful in the day just as you are in the night.

You are as beautiful in your strength as you are in your darkness.

You are the most beautiful you possible!

You become more beautiful each moment you live!

Beautiful you!

Now go be you and live!

-BonniferWW

Imagine buying your dream car......or winning big on the lottery.....or being given your dream home.....or winning your dream vacation.....or......or......or......BUT you're not allowed to tell anyone about it EVER! Like your mouth is duct taped shut about it. Would you do it? Of course you say yes, but I'm being serious here. Could you do it? Could you actually do it? Could you do it without lying? You drive up to work in a new Lamborghini. What are you going to say? "Can't talk about it". Then there's all of the never ending questions coming to that statement, but you know that. What would you do?

 Now what if you had your dream car or house or vacation, you weren't allowed to tell anyone about it, AND for one year you'd also stutter. How bad of a stutter? I cannot tell you that. No one knows the answer to that question. Why stuttering? Honestly? Because people think that others with a disability, whether it's small or huge, aren't supposed to have nice things. This time, it's something relatively small on the grand scheme of things.

Would you still take that vacation? That dream house? Car?
This is my guess. If you are an outgoing type A personality
person, you would not survive well, if at all, on any of the gift
choices above. On the other hand, if you are a type B
personality, are shy, etc then you would probably have a 5
gold star rating on your choice of gifts. In fact, you'd finish
one and ask where you could sign up for the next silence
competition. (Even if there was no prize…. maybe.)

What's the point of this? Hang on…we just started the
chapter. Sheesh! What if you had a zillion things going on in
your head and around you, but you didn't know how to share
them with people. Then when you tried, some laughed at
you. Some turned away. Some just said you were snobby
because you were quiet. When you tried, you were told to be
quiet by your parents because they spoke for you. When you
tried to express yourself, you were laughed at by your
parents. When you tried to "talk" in other forms, (writing is
one) you were told by your parents it isn't good enough.

This "what if" isn't a "what if". It really happened in my life.
It's more of what I grew up in. It became obvious early on
that it was easier to just stay quiet. I had my twin sister
anyway to talk to. I didn't need an adult to talk to most of the
time.

When Mom would take us to the doctor, which was rare
anyway, she always did basically all of the talking. Even as
older children, I remember the nurse or doctor looking at me
talking, but it was Mom that answered. One time we came
home from a doctor appointment and Mom was mad. We
asked why. She said because the doctor had made a remark

that there was something wrong with us because we weren't developing normal speed. This was due to our not talking much at all.

At family gatherings, I'd be found in the kitchen washing dishes. Not spending time with my grandparents. Not spending time with aunts and uncles and cousins. But washing dishes. To this day, I have many extended family members I barely know because of this. But on the other hand, washing the dishes doesn't take much talking either. You don't have to worry about what you're going to say next in a conversation or what someone is going to think about what you say. You can just be.

In school, from kindergarten through third grade, we went to schools that used a pace system. Basically it was thin booklets that the student works through on his own. The teacher is there to monitor, answer questions, and keep the student on track. So basically, to some extent, the student teaches himself. With this type of schooling, there was less interaction with classmates and adults. Less need for communication. Then beginning in fourth grade, we began at a more traditional school with the typical classrooms and instruction. How do you learn to communicate suddenly that late? Then Mom and Dad are already speaking for me too. That became even more. Later on in Junior high and high school, Mom would even call classmates for questions on assignments and such. I wasn't allowed too. Yes, I know.

In a time of life, when one should be talking to and about boys, I wasn't allowed to talk to them outside of the classroom. The parents sure kept a close eye on me. It seemed as if it was so that I wouldn't talk to anyone about what was going on at home. But even if I had the opportunity, I don't think I would have known how to. I don't think I would have had the words to describe the situation. When you don't talk much, for whatever reason, it's going to be extremely difficult to talk to another human being.

I talked little. Sometimes Mom and dad forced me to tell them my opinion about things, but then they would just laugh. So again, why talk. Tears became my emotional outlet. Dad's response to the tears? "Turn off the tears or I'll give you something to cry about."

When I did talk, I remember it being repetitive of conversations before. It was safe that way. My dream wedding was a popular topic of conversation to have with Mom. Otherwise it was talk about school or chores and such. I remember the conversation being juvenile. When I used a more mature word, the parents would again laugh. They judged how I prayed before supper and would tell me how I needed to change it. Again, if I don't talk, then I don't get judged.

But of course there's the other side of the coin. By not being able to or learning to speak, life was a bit more difficult. For whatever reason, Mom and Dad suddenly decided that we weren't participating in classes at school enough. So they made this chart that we had to have the teacher sign if we participated or not. Do you know how humiliating that is? I quickly learned there were no consequences at home. Plus the whole thing didn't last long anyway. If something took extra effort and time on Mom and Dad's part, it most likely wouldn't last all that long.

Then there was speech class both in high school and in college. It was all I could do just to pass either one. Of course high school speech was less pressure, but I sure didn't know that at the time. College speech was absolutely horrible. I felt like I could do nothing correctly in those speeches. I was lucky if I got a C.

I was scared to ask an employee where something was in the grocery store. Why? First, Mom had always done it. Second, when she'd send us to the store for a list of things and we'd come back with stuff, if we told her we had to ask where something was, she'd make fun of us for having to ask where something was. As in, "Oh wow! You mean you actually asked someone. You talked to a stranger?" That type of ridiculousness.

Many times, people would think of me as stuck up or goody two shoes because I was so quiet and shy. But they didn't take the time to get to know me either. You know the saying "Don't judge a book by the cover".

So what did I do? How did I handle it? Well, I subconsciously explored my options. In my sophomore year of college, I took a First Responder course. I originally took it because I wanted to know what to do in an emergency. But little did I know how much it would change my life. Small choices like that can change your life path forever. I grew from there in EMS. My shyness slowly became easier to deal with. Yes, I am still shy. Yes, it is still a struggle. But it's doable now.

I've found that writing is my outlet. I still don't always talk much. I'm still quiet. I still struggle for words, even more so now with my injuries. But when I write, I've found that words are my friend. Words come to me like never before imagined. Words just flow when I write. Before that incident, I couldn't write like this. Sure I tried, but it wasn't like this.

I think what I'm trying to say here is that if you are the shy one, don't give up. No matter the reason you're shy. Even if it's because you are an introvert and no other reason. If you want to change it, you can. It's possible. It doesn't have to be as drastic as a career change, but maybe a new hobby or fulfilling that dream you've been ignoring or even writing a book yourself. You can do it!

Chapter 8

Beginning of EMS Life

What is?

What is your one goal?

That dream.

That secret.

That one thing.

That one thing that you think about often.

Money? Happiness? Love? Fame?

What is that thing that makes you get out of bed every morning?

Chasing that promotion?

Chasing that "true love"?

Chasing that next big thing?

That one thing that you think about often.

Dream vacation? Travel? Kids? Worry free life?

What is it that makes life truly worth living?

What if you're lonely? Is it still worth living?

What if you struggle to make ends meet? Is it still worth living?

What if you feel a failure? Is it still worth living?

What if you were to lose a close friend/family member? Is it still worth living?

What if the "what if" didn't exist? What if you just were? What then?

What if you were to lose everything you have?

What if you were to lose everyone you know?

What if you lost the way you see and know life as it is now?

What if you had to face the worst possible imaginable circumstances?

And you survived?

What then?

Would you still have the same worries?

Would you still have the same goals?

Would you still have the same dreams?

Would you still have the same priorities?

What if goals, dreams, and priorities became goals, dreams, and priorities that were valuable?

What if goals, dreams, and priorities would grow as we grow?

What if no matter what life threw, you knew those goals, dreams, and priorities would still be there?

Love a little stronger.

Laugh a little longer.

Be a little more there.

Live like this moment was your last.

-BonniferWW

As a young child, I had wanted to be a "mad scientist" when I grew up. I'd even dress up as one for contests at school or Halloween. The long white lab coat. The white goggles. The test tubes. There was a guy at church that let me borrow some stuff from where he worked for these days. I was in heaven. One year for Christmas, I even received a chemistry set. Yep, it was pretty dang awesome. Well, in a roundabout way, it kind of turned out that way.

Back to that First Responder course I had taken in college........I had no clue what to do to help someone in a time of need and I also had no clue what I was getting into as far as choosing this career either. I thought the class was CPR and a band aid course. In reality, it was so much more. It was that but it was assessing the situation to be able to know what the problem is in order to know what to do. Back then, that was huge in my life. I wasn't able to do that really in any part of my life. This course would end up teaching me and preparing me for so much more than I ever could have imagined.

At the end of that course, I was a First Responder now. I was ready to save the world. Sure felt like I was anyhow. I wanted a First Aid kit for Christmas that year, but it had to have a few more things in it than what you typically buy in the store. Plus it had to have a few particular items too. Mostly certain size items that we had used in class or bottles of water to be able to "rinse a wound" if need be. Those types of things.

Every time I heard sirens I got goosebumps. Every time I saw someone slip and fall, I asked if they were okay or needed help. If I was at a distance, I watched to make sure they got up okay. I was ready to help at the drop of a hat. Now I would have helped anyway, but now I had this reason also. It wasn't that I wanted someone to get hurt, but if they did…. or when they did….I wanted to be there.

I continued with my college classes. As time progressed though, I slowly got to the point where I wanted to be able to do more to help people. I wanted to be able to be on that ambulance helping others. Learning to cook and sew and all was great, but at the rate I was going, I knew I wasn't going to be getting married anytime soon. I already knew the basics and then some, so I surely wasn't going to starve living on my own. Plus I had no desire to teach Home Economics either. This college only had majors for those who wanted to be Pastors, missionaries, teachers, or "MRS degree" aka Home Economics. I wasn't majoring in Home Economics for that reason. It was just something I enjoyed, and I had to pick something. So why was I continuing with this major anyway? Oh yeah…...the parents. But we discussed that already in a previous chapter. So I won't bore you with details again.

I decided to stick with the classes and finish school. My sister had taken this course a year later and had decided to drop out to continue on the EMS track. The parents had a raging fit to say the least. I knew I could start as soon as I graduated.

I ended up graduating college in May of 2002 even though I had actually finished in the Fall of 2001. Small schools and one-time annual graduations. My sister and I moved out on our own in Spring of 2003 and I began Basic EMT school in August of 2003.

By the time I was doing EMT basic clinicals, Yoana was beginning to do her Paramedic clinicals in the emergency room. Great! Cool! Well, my first ER clinical, I was scared to pieces. Nobody introduced themselves. Nobody showed me around. Nobody did anything. I had heard all these wonderful things from classmates about the staff, but I was getting none of it. "Oh they are so helpful." "They showed me how to do this when I wasn't sure about it." "Oh guess what! I got to see an epidural done!" What was wrong with me? Why was I the one to be ignored? What was happening?

Oh yeah! I have a twin! Yes, you laugh. I laugh now, too. But then I probably cried…….in the bathroom.…..maybe even the blubbery cry because I was so frustrated and scared and nervous. Remember I was still extremely terribly shy at this point. The staff thought I was Yoana and didn't know I was her sister. No wonder they kept asking me to go do IV's and then giving me weird looks when I told them I wasn't allowed to do those. Oh how they laughed. Word traveled fast. It didn't take long before I didn't have to worry about telling them I couldn't do IV's anymore. Of course I didn't have to do that many clinical hours either. I was done pretty quickly.

I was a real EMT by the beginning of 2004. Holy Crap!!!! If you thought I was excited over being a First Responder, you should have seen me over being an EMT. If you've never seen the movie "Ambulance Girl", you should watch it. It describes me perfectly at this point. It's about a middle-aged woman having a midlife crisis who ends up deciding to be an EMT. Yep. She is so excited when she finishes that she makes her own emergency bag for her vehicle, buys stuff off the internet to add to it, drives her hubby insane responding to every possible call that came out...............describes me to an absolute T. Ha-ha!

I spent several years as an EMT. Not even sure now how many years, but it was over 5 years. The time does include the time it took to go through Paramedic school and past national registry. Oh I learned and grew so much. I went from being a shy little girl to being a shy young woman. That wouldn't make sense to just anyone, but I hope that after reading this far, that it makes sense to you the reader. Sure, my extent of experience as an EMT was working in the ER and time as a Volunteer EMT. During that time, I ran every possible call I could. I did a lot of ambulance driving, a lot of assisting paramedics, and some of running my own calls. Of course, the time in the ER helped too because I was learning skills there too. I also triaged every patient that came in the door. So there's that assessment skill right there.

Back then I didn't know it of course, but now I can plainly see it. I was taught by old school paramedics for which I'm very thankful for. Most today are taught like the coffee at Starbucks - make them look good, make them look knowledgeable, make them look skilled.....but don't worry about the taste. In actuality, they should be concerned about the presentation and the taste. Add in patient care with TLC. (I'm not a Starbucks fan. Can you tell? Ha-ha! Love you anyway!) But being a great EMT or Paramedic is so much more than that. It has to come from the soul and innermost being possible. EMS is really a calling.

The EMS bug bit me during the First Responder course and I've never recovered. This is not something you do because you "want to help people " or because you "want to play with sirens' ' or because you "want to see blood and guts". Yes, those are parts of this, but it's truly a calling. If you weren't called to do this, you will not survive. You see, hear, and feel things that no human was made to go through. Hence the reason, or one reason, for the cause of PTSD. We weren't made for this, but a few of us were called for this. I still struggle with things I've seen and dealt with from years ago, but I wouldn't have traded this job for the world. Many older EMT's and Paramedics, when asked by the younger generation for advice about beginning their EMS careers, will tell them to not get into this career and to avoid it at all costs. The low pay and long hours, the impending back problems that come with the years of EMS, exposure to numerous chemicals and diseases, the things you see and deal with has a forever lasting impression on you, and oh so much more. Even if I had known this beforehand, I still would have chosen this career.

Chapter 9

EGH ER Tech and More EMS Stories

Granted!

Don't take for granted your next breath.

For it could be your end.

Don't take for granted your ability to walk.

For your next step could be your last.

Don't take for granted your thoughts.

For that thought could become scrambled.

Don't take for granted your love of life.

For your life could end in a moment.

Don't take for granted your friends in your life.

For they could turn their backs when life gets rough.

Don't take for granted your family.

For they could show they don't truly care.

Don't take for granted your ability to work.

For you could become disabled in an instant.

Don't take for granted your skill of driving.

For lack of response time could take your license.

Don't take for granted your love of participating in sports.

For you may no longer be able to run.

Don't take for granted your sight.

For it could be affected by many a cause.

Don't take for granted your hearing.

For you could no longer be able to hear the birds chirping.

Love life in the way you know it.

Live life for what you make it.

Laugh at your own self for what you have done.

Life is what you make it.

Life is a privilege.

Life is to be lived to the best of your ability.

Life is meant to help someone else.

Sometimes life sucks.

Sometimes life is draining.

Sometimes life is depressing.

But sunshine will always come.

But the light is just around the corner.

But the rewards are in the future.

Never give up.

Never give in.

For it's five minutes at a time.

-BonniferWW

Please bear with me for a minute. Sometimes stories from the world of EMS can be filled with details worse than an R rated movie. Yes really! Since this book is not R rated, nor is it written to be, this chapter will remain G rated. So please keep that in mind when considering skipping this chapter. Also, no HIPAA laws have been broken. No identifying information is given. Any possible identifying information has been changed to not be identifying information. This includes sex, circumstances, and any other information protected by HIPAA.

Please do not skip this chapter. This is just a heads up. If you are easily grossed out, then you may want to skip this chapter, but please don't. I promise that it will not be utterly disgusting and gross. There will be a few details, but it will not be very descriptive. If it gets too much, then please move ahead to the next chapter. Deal? Deal.

I began working in the emergency room as a brand new "baby" EMT. I had no experience in the medical field whatsoever. I also had never seen a dead person outside of the funeral home. I had never taken a rectal temperature on a baby. I had never even been called nasty names by rude people. Oh how I had so much growing up to do.

It was in the first week on the job when the charge nurse sent me to the trauma room to clean up the patient so that the family could say their goodbyes. The patient had passed and needed to have tubes and wires pulled, fluids wiped away, a clean gown placed, etc. I walked in the room and looked around. I was scared spitless. I had never touched someone who was dead before. I tried to begin working. Breathe! I worked to concentrate on what I was doing instead of who I was doing it to and the circumstances around it. The hands on the clock on the wall seemed to stand still. The room was really hot. I felt like I couldn't breathe. Just at that moment, Ginger, the charge nurse, stuck her head in the room to check on me. She took one look at me and gave me a different job to do. I don't think I could have gotten out of there any faster. I was so very relieved.

I was working nights. At this time, I sat out front and would triage and check patients in. There was a patient who weighed almost 500 pounds and was one of the many who, for whatever circumstances and reasons, used the emergency room as their primary care physician. Typically this patient was known for not being the most nice, nor the most easy-going patient in the waiting room. This one would walk inside just fine from the car, then sit in a wheelchair, and demand that staff push him/her around.......to the coffee pot, the restroom, etc. It didn't matter if we were empty or running our tooshies off. (Many patients are like this, not just this one.)

On this particular visit, it was for a sleep study. After the patient was registered, it was my job to wheel him/her upstairs to the lab. Wheeling that kind of weight is much easier on tile than it is on carpet. That night it was on carpet - which means the point where you need to go is the point in the corner farthest away. By the time, I made it back, my low back was hurting really bad. When I could, I hid in the corner and did some stretching. But after a few hours when my low back pain was only getting worse, I finally said something to the charge nurse. You know the drill: paperwork, see the doctor, pee in a cup, etc. I was on light duty for a couple of weeks. When the pain worsened, the doctor sent me for massages a few times a week along with the physical therapy. When I still wasn't improving after a few weeks of this added course of treatment, my massage therapist told me that it was the light duty that was making things worse because light duty was doing things using the exact muscles that had been injured. That massage therapist was really HOT too by the way. I may or may not have continued going to him for a much longer extended period of time after the injury had healed. Wink.

Another night shift story. The hospital was remodeling the triage area. There was no parking up by the drop off door now with the construction. It was just a circle drive with a drop off point. There was a ramp up to the door with no other option to get up to the entrance. It was a steep ramp too. So after a certain point at night, I was the only one out there. Sometimes security would be out there too, but only if they weren't busy. This particular time, I was alone.

There were a couple people out there chilling while they waited with their family member, who was in the emergency room, for test results. All of a sudden, the lady of the couple burst through the doors yelling at me that someone had just collapsed out there. The man of the couple grabbed a wheelchair. I called for security to bring a gurney and help from the back. I checked the patient for respirations and a pulse. When there was none, the three of us picked up the man and put him in the wheelchair. As we brought him inside and around the corner, there came a full crew of security and emergency staff in sight. We again picked up the patient, put him on the gurney, and instantly began CPR and other life sustaining procedures needed. I had to go back out front and man my post, but my mind was on what had just happened. Would a life be saved? Would that life be able to walk out of this hospital or would it be machine dependable for years on? Or would the Grim Reaper simply win another fight?

I worked at this hospital for several years. In that time, I hurt my back, I had a super mild rash they thought was chicken pox. I got 2 weeks off work with pay for it. It wasn't and I still haven't had chicken pox even after all these years doing this job. I also somehow got Mono from a patient too.

There are fun times, bad times, great times, sucky times, times to celebrate, times for tears, time to smile, times to mourn, times for hugs, times to rejoice, and times to be glad the shift is finally over. I learned so much from each of my patients. The good and the beautiful, and even the ugly and mean.

What happened to the patient who tried to die on the emergency doorstep? Approximately 45 minutes later, one of the security guards came out front to let me know that they had got him/her to the catheter lab, had come through strongly, and was expected to make a great recovery. We both high-fived! I went home that morning flying on clouds.

Chapter 10

Paramedic School

Struggling!

I'm struggling.

I'm struggling hard...

To stay afloat

To be positive

To keep my head up.

How much longer must I endure these struggles?

How much more negative events must I carry?

I'm struggling.

I'm struggling hard…

To keep from crying

To keep a smile on my face

To keep pushing forward.

How much more can I take?

How much longer must I carry this load?

I'm struggling.

I'm struggling hard…

To work through these emotions

To make myself get out of bed each day

To not return the ugly that I have received.

How much more darkness must I face?

How much more? Longer? Darker?

I feel very alone, but I know I'm far from alone.

I feel very low even though I am being carried through.

I see all darkness even though that darkness is surrounded by light.

I feel heavily weighed down but know that I will finish this race, too.

Someday! Somehow! Somewhere! There will be a victory party.

-BonniferWW

Sometimes after being in a job for a while, you decide you want more training or advancement. Sometimes you decide you want more skills or cross-training. Sometimes you want to be able to do more in the same thing in order to help others more. Now for me personally? I don't like being stuck in a rut, monotonous, boring, every day is the same type of thing. I wanted to be able to help people yes, but it was more than that. I wanted to learn more of the anatomy and physiology behind it, but I also wanted to be able to take my patient care to a higher level. I didn't want to have to drive the ambulance. I was horrible at directional. Knowing where you're going is NOT the paramedics job. Haha.

After I'd been an EMT for a few years, I began thinking about Paramedic school. Prior to this, whenever the Paramedic instructor would see me, he'd ask when I was going to sign up for class. I'd mutter something or other to get out of it. But then he started to get serious about getting me in class. I told him I wasn't even confident in taking a manual blood pressure so how am I going to be a paramedic. He just smiled and said that we'd work on it. Those words "We'll work on it" were words I'd hear several more times throughout the course of class.

I signed up and turned in all the paperwork required. Now to just sit and wait and sweat. What am I thinking? Can I really be a paramedic? Then someone would come along and tell me that if my sister made it through, that I definitely could make it too. Nerves would calm for a half second maybe, but then would be full blown worked up again. Things stayed this way until the first night of class.

We had a good 20 books, clinical shirts, and I don't remember what else I came home with that first night. It was rather impressive though......and intimidating. Tony, the instructor, had given us all the ins and outs of class. The expectations were great and the assignments were nerve racking for me.

We had to do 20 live intubations in the OR. 350 hours on the ambulance, 350 hours in the emergency room, and the rest was many other departments for clinicals. Those three were the biggest. There was class 2 nights a week with some Saturdays too. This was all done in 18 months. EVERYTHING!

I had major trouble getting the OR staff to let me even attempt to intubate. They would tell me things like "oh it's a hard one" or "It's a conscious sedation" or "It's an LMA not an ET tube, so I'll do it".....'i'll do it"...."I'll do it"... I'd ask about every single case, then get looked at like I was the weird kid picking my nose or something. When it was an OR clinical day, I would get so stressed out, I would get physically ill. One day, I couldn't take it anymore and called off sick from an OR clinical, but had class that night. At class that night, Tony called me into his office to ask if I was okay. It wasn't like me to call off a clinical. I told him what was going on. He said he'd talk to the head of the OR staff. The next time I went in, it was a completely different atmosphere. People were welcoming. I was encouraged to go into rooms. My first successful ET intubation, we all cheered. My confidence began to rise.

I had one anesthesiologist that I did several intubations with and a few of those were older kids. On my last shift and on what would be my 20th intubation, he had a pediatric patient he let me intubate. It was an age that no one else in my class had gotten to intubate while in the OR. I was rather stoked. I'd rather have the experience of intubating that young age under close supervision of majorly experienced trained eyes than to have to do it the first time out in the field with no one around.

Class was going well. I was feeling like I was a part of the gang. Our class was becoming very close knit. Almost every night after class, we'd go across the street to one of the few restaurants there to get a bite to eat and hang out for a bit. I went most of the time. Plus every once in a great while, we'd have a get together at someone's house. It would involve food, fun, and alcohol. The cops were never called. Honest!

Now, at the beginning of this whole paramedic class venture, I was unable to say body parts. What? Yes, I could verbally say the basic body parts. If it was genitalia or even having to do with the breasts or the pelvis area, I seriously struggled to be able to say the word. Many things were taboo topics at home and so were saying certain words. Every so often in class, I would get teased about saying the word "nipple". So I just decided it needed to be done. It's emergency medicine, I'm going to be a Paramedic, and I'm almost 30 years old. It's past time. The next night in class, when there was a long break in Tony lecturing, students' responses, and the usual smartass comments, I shyly and in a voice twice as loud as a mouse, I simply said "Nipple". There was a second of silence, then Tony asked me to repeat myself. I was instantly beat red. I couldn't say it again, but I had to. I said it again, a little louder "Nipple". The entire class roared with laughter. The class bought my drink and food that night.

I love professional clowns (the good professional clowns) and I used to be one. That's all another story though. Because of that, I used to have a hard plastic red nose on the front end of my car. Had one there for several years. I hit a deer one time. The first thing out of my mouth was that the deer had broken the clown nose. Not the damage to the vehicle or if I was injured or not or whatever. Nope. Clown nose is all important. Haha! So one night I told Tony that I was going to be a little late to class. Yoana and I timed it so that we'd have enough time between the last person going in late to class and the first break. We zip tied a clown nose to the hood of each classmate's vehicle that night. Yes, everyone had a clown nose.

A short time later, I noticed that my clown nose was not on my car. Gone! Missing! Oh I was so mad! I narrowed it down to someone at school who had taken him. They had literally cut him from my car and then who knows what. I made all sorts of remarks that were only met with smiling eyes. That only made me all the more mad.

Then it started. I went to class and received a copy of a passport that had "Mister Red Nose" in the name box. I was mad, but I had to laugh. At least I knew he was okay. Then periodically during Tony's lecture's, he would have a random power-point slide that would pop up and it would be a picture of Mister Red Nose in his travels around the world.

It really was hilarious and very creative. It was frustrating because nobody would tell me who had actually taken him off my car in the first place. Also frustrating because nobody would tell me when he would be safely returned. Mister Red Nose ended up with his own email and own MySpace page too. He was FINALLY returned during our graduation ceremony. Yes, during the ceremony. He was well traveled, still in great condition, and even had his nose pierced. Yes, a nose had his nose pierced.

The grading system in paramedic school is a little different than typical. If your average drops below 80% during a unit at any time, then you are out of the program. Buh bye. So it sure keeps you on your toes. Tony would let his students retake a test once to be able to keep a score up. I had been doing halfway decent so far. I struggled. There were tears, but I got through it. But then there was cardiology. Cardiology was a unit that was done more than halfway through the course. We had been in the cardiology unit for a good while when I finally came to the decision that I just needed to stay an EMT, that some people weren't cut out to be paramedics and I was one of them, that if I couldn't interpret a heart rhythm then I had no business trying to be a paramedic.

I went to class early that night with all the books, clinical shirts and everything else for class loaded in my car. I was going to turn everything in and quit paramedic school. My mind was made up. I walked into Tony's office that night with an armload. He took one look at me, shooed everyone out of his office, told me to sit, and asked me what was up. I told him everything. The tears just fell. The frustration, the anger, the feelings of failure. We talked a good while. He somehow talked me into staying and said those words "We'll work on it". Then he got this comical but still caring look on his face. I asked him what that look was for. He told me that Yoana had wanted to quit too about the same spot and thought it was very interesting.

It was during paramedic school that I had to have a tonsillectomy. During the surgery, the surgeon was in a hurry and nicked a branch of the carotid artery. I lost two units of blood and had to stay in the hospital much longer. He wanted to keep me longer than necessary, but I told him I'd get better care at home. Also, if something in an emergency fashion happened, he sure wasn't going to touch me again. The nurses were often two hours late on pain meds too. So I made arrangements to stay at a friend's house (also a paramedic school classmate) who worked in an OR. She had talked to every specialist I would need if an emergency happened for my case. Then I signed myself out of the hospital. The doctor wasn't happy, very nervous, and gave me far more pain meds than I would ever need. Recovery went fine though.

I was also in paramedic school when I had that bout of Mono that I mentioned in a previous chapter. Was I sure this was the right time to do paramedic school? Maybe I shouldn't do the paramedic thing at all. Was I doing the wrong thing? Well, two paramedics that I worked with on the volunteer service took me out for lunch one day to discuss that very thing. They highly suggested that I drop out of school and wait until the next class started. Then try again. At that moment, I only told them maybe and that I would think about it. But in reality, it only made me more determined to stick with it. Just because there's a storm or even a few storms, doesn't mean that you decide to move to a different state. NO! You stay put. You dig down your roots. Can you imagine what would happen if a tree would give up every time the wind would blow a little rough? Or the raindrops were bigger than normal? Or the ice accumulation was a bit more than normal? Now obviously trees, when planted and taken care of properly, don't give up easily. So why in tarnation would I give up over some health issues? I was still going. I wasn't dying. I sure wasn't struggling to keep going either. I hadn't even been seriously considering quitting. But here now, these two were telling me to quit. What the hell! This all just made me more determined to finish.

The memories of the 18 months of paramedic school are endless. The sweat, blood, and tears seemed to be nonstop at times. The laughter, the comradery, and the closeness we had as a class. The strides I made personally in my own life had been enormous. I had gone from not being able to say "nipple" without major blushing to being able to run a male genitalia call and say male genitalia words in the radio report. How's that for improvement? A+ right there.

On a serious note, many people had told me to not to. Many people told me I couldn't. Many people had tried to interfere.

But if you know deep down that it is what you are supposed to do, it is where you are supposed to be, and it is the thing that you have dreamed to do, then go after it. If it's right and you know it's right, go do it! This goes if you believe in God, believe in nothing, believe in nature, or something or someone else.

Okay, one more story. When I found this pair of shorts with a fake butt in the back, I knew it would be totally perfect for some future prank with my class. I ended up deciding to save them for the class graduation party. Prior to paramedic school, I wasn't one to cuss or swear. One night in class, Tony had been teasing me (all in good fun) relentlessly about something. It went on and on. Then all of a sudden, right out in the middle of class, I called Tony an "Assbutt!" (I have no clue why that combination of words.) The entire class stopped and for a split second, it was so quiet in there, you could have heard a pin drop. But then Tony and the entire class broke in roaring laughter.

At our private graduation party, I had slipped away and pulled on the shorts under my clothes to be ready. Us girls were going to shock the guys. We were seated in a big circle with food and drinks sharing memories. The other girls and I had it planned to talk about the original "assbutt" incident and then I would get up and flash everyone. The plan went perfect. The ending? Consisted of our whole class rolling with laughter. Seriously rolling.

Chapter 11

Working as a Paramedic in Indiana

The Dark Hole

This dark hole that I find myself in...

What is it? How long must I be here? How deep does this go?

This dark deep hole I find myself in...

Is there a way out of here? Where is the door that leads to the sunshine I am used to?

This dark deep hole I find myself in...

Is there a purpose for me being here? How do I find that purpose?

This dark deep hole I find myself in...

Someday it will lead me to the sunshine.

Someday I will see the purpose for all of my suffering.

Someday I will be stronger for the battles I have fought.

Until then...

I will pick my head up AGAIN.

I will brush the dirt off my skinned knees AGAIN.

I will bandage my wounds AGAIN.

I will stand up strong AGAIN.

I will lean on those who are my strength through these battles AGAIN.

Until then...

Never give up.

Until then...

Never give up through the storms.

Until then...

Never give up in the darkest of time.

For in your darkest hour, you ARE someone else's strength.

-BonniferWW

School is FINALLY finished! Now I can go find a paramedic job and start working as a paramedic right!?!?!?!? Well, that was the plan. But the plan doesn't always get executed the way it's planned. I wish the plan would go off without a hitch, but no, it doesn't. It sure didn't this time either.

After passing the class written and the class skills, one must then pass the National Registry Written and also the National Registry Skills. I did everything above without a hitch except for the National Registry written. It took me four times to pass that thing. It had also taken Yoana four times to pass the written test, too.

Toward the end of Paramedic school, I applied to the Lawrence Township Fire Department in Indianapolis. The first part of the application was a written test. I was applying as an EMT since I was still in school, but I only had three months left. I received a 100% on the test. Tony's response was "What? Just writing your name?" Apparently, the Indianapolis fire department had never had someone get a 100% on that test before because they made a big deal about it. Plus that's what they told me. I still have trouble believing it though.

I made it through the written and through the interviews. Then I got the phone call offering me the job. I was ecstatic. Never in my dreams did I think I'd actually get that job. Holy crap!!! Now I had to turn in my notice at my current job. That was not going to be enjoyable…..the two places who basically took me from a preemie EMT and began teaching me the real stuff. You don't learn a lot of the real stuff until you're out of the classroom. Leaving those two jobs were very sad difficult days. I don't do well with goodbyes.

I began my new job at LTFD. Only thing is that in that first week, I had three different guys come to me separately to tell me to watch my back. They said that the chief didn't like females on that shift and had a history of getting rid of them. Fabulous! Why did I get picked for this shift at this firehouse then? I loved the guys I worked with.

Then the harassment started. I would get called into the lieutenant's office almost every shift. He would tell me I wasn't being assertive enough or something was wrong with my narrative or I took a blood pressure wrong. The ambulance and fire truck would respond to all calls. So it's me assessing the patient with six guys just standing there watching me. In the beginning weeks, my EMT would help me. But in the later weeks, the lieutenant even had my EMT stand back. I was supposed to tell each of them what to do step by step on a call while on a call. Then when I tried to do that, I was told to "never mind" or "hang on" and they would do it their own way. I knew very quickly that I was on my way out. I also knew I was going to fight to the death because I was not in the wrong.

Now if I had the mouth and confidence back then that I have now, this story could quite possibly have a different outcome. But I didn't and I still allowed people to walk on me by the multitudes. When the constant harassment by the lieutenant didn't work, I was moved to a different station.

The attitudes, atmosphere, and everything was very different here. It was very Type A personality driven and everyone was out only for themselves. I wasn't allowed to help wash the trucks. In fact, I was told to clean up the kitchen after supper while the guys washed the trucks. This was on multiple occasions. The lieutenant at this station called me into his office a couple times, almost begging me to quit. He offered me severance packages, too; two weeks' pay, great references - the works! I refused and told him that I'm too stubborn to quit. I knew exactly what was happening to me, but at the time, I didn't have the guts to say it. I should have gone to human resources and filed complaints for sexual harassment, but I didn't. I was doing nothing wrong. Only wrong was that I had a vagina and boobs.

This place had been odd from the get-go. I had been given uniforms from the beginning, but my sweatpants had been printed backwards. They refused to fix those. I had never been given a locker because they claimed they didn't have any available. They claimed that my winter coat was back-ordered, but I never received one. Late fall, I called the uniform shop to check on it and was told it had never been ordered.

I had been hired in June, but I was fired in December right before Christmas. I went in for my shift. I was told we were going to the other station because I had a meeting with the chief. I knew then what was happening. Sure enough, I went up to his office. I was told that basically I didn't know what I was doing and blah blah blah. I sat there with tears streaming down my face wanting badly to defend myself, but unable to say a word. I wasn't given a chance to say a word. Just a "sign here" and a "bring in your uniforms before you receive your last paycheck". I bawled my eyes out all the way to the car and a good portion of the way home.

During this time, I was still trying to pass the National Registry written. I decided to take three months of unemployment to study for that test. I studied two hours a day minimum, no matter what. I bought a book of questions, read them onto a recorder, then listened to it constantly when I wasn't studying. All of this finally paid off to help me pass.

Now I must find a job. There are multiple help wanted ads for paramedics at multiple services in probably almost any state you would want to live, Indiana included. I applied to several in Indiana. Only thing is that these places want you to have experience too…..at least in Indiana they did. I could not find a job for anything as a paramedic. So I found a job as an EMT at Family Mobile doing transfers, mostly for dialysis. I was fine with it. I loved my patients and most of the people I worked with. On the first day of orientation there was this blonde-haired guy that was very handsome in the way he looked and in the way he carried himself. He, Josh, even talked to me. One of the first days on the truck, we were all clocking out for the day. He asked me for my phone number. I told him it was 9-1-1. I've had guys ask for my number before and most of the time, they don't seriously want it. When I tell them 9-1-1, they laugh and walk away. It gets rid of them basically.

The next morning, also at the time clock, Josh stopped me again to ask me for my number. I again told him it was 9-1-1, but he would have none of it. He still had to clock in but told me to not go anywhere. I laughed. Maybe I had made this guy work hard enough. Maybe he really did want my number. I was nice and gave it to him. To this day, Josh and I are still friends. When he was overseas in the military, I sent him cards and cookies. When I drove up to Montana several years ago for a half-marathon, he rode his bike out there from Washington state to support me. You never know what giving someone your phone number will do.

The job at Family Mobile didn't last very long because paychecks began bouncing. I was out! It was okay though because I had just been hired at a hospital in Rochester, Indiana. I was stoked! My very first paramedic job. Yoana had also worked here for a couple years a while before me. Being the cuter twin…..and the better overall twin anyhow…..ha-ha!

The hospital ran the ambulance service for the county. The medical director held very high expectations of his EMS personnel. I worked in the emergency room when not on a call. This was very cool because I was able to work with and see the rest of the story of my patient. Otherwise, it's just a drop off the patient and leave having no contact ever again (most likely) with that patient to know the outcome. Sometimes it was difficult working in both the emergency room and on the ambulance because you didn't get a break after a rough call, but on the other side of the coin, there were always things to do after a rough call. I grew much in my confidence here.

After a couple of years here, the county decided they could operate the ambulance service better than the hospital and took things over. The medical director also changed personnel. Things went downhill quickly. The reputation, the attitude, the skill level, the respect, competence, everything. The manager, Beatrice, the county hired basically ran off all the good medics or all the medics that weren't on her favorites list. Literally!

First she started knit picking my calls - such as telling me I intubated too soon. How can you begin breathing for the patient too soon right? I also had a burn patient who had approximately 12% of their body covered with second degree burns. The patient refused pain medication and I had to talk the patient into accepting it. Beatrice told me that I should have "snowed" the patient. In other words, I should have drugged so highly that the patient was seriously drugged almost to the point of being delirious. Only thing is, we didn't have protocols for burns so that I couldn't have done it even if I wanted to. Only way I could have is if I had called in to the emergency department to ask the doctor for orders. It isn't necessary, especially when it's being refused by the patient. Plus we weren't that far from the hospital. I went and talked to the medical director about it, but Beatrice had already gotten a hold of him. It was quite obvious that he didn't even have the balls to stand up to her and we were practicing under his medical license. He told me that whatever happened to me was up to Beatrice, not him. HELLO! No, actually it's up to the medical director what the EMS protocols are and what the consequences are when the protocols are not followed. Beatrice then cut my hours in half telling me I needed to go volunteer hours (yes, for free) with a particular service to gain experience. I didn't argue or say a word because I had a job interview scheduled in Tulsa, Oklahoma. If that interview had not been successful, then I would have come back and raised a ruckus. But instead, after I came back from the trip to Oklahoma, (I kept the trip a secret) I calmly handed her my resignation letter and told her to give me my vacation hours the next pay period. She may have thought she had won, but to me, I was the winner. I was moving up in the world and I was getting there honestly.

Chapter 12

Climate Change - Move to Oklahoma

I am learning.

I am learning to put one foot in front of the other. Sometimes that means crawling, but it's still one foot at a time moving forward.

I am learning to love all...even those who are rude or nasty or hateful towards me.

I am learning that words are only that. Actions speak much louder. True intentions will always be found out.

I am learning to accept others' help. I am in a period of time where I need to be helped instead of being the one to help.

I am learning that in my darkest hour, I can lean on the strength of those around me, I can still be an encouragement when I am struggling. There is still a purpose to my suffering.

I am learning what true physical pain is. There is pain and THEN there is pain. There will always be pain in this life. Learn to accept it. Grow from it. Dig through it. Don't let it keep you from reaching your goals. Let it encourage you instead.

I am learning to be patient and be a patient. It totally sucks! But this too will make me stronger. It will give me so much better understanding with my future patients. Life's trials have always done that for me. In every single instance, I have later been able to help/encourage a patient because of what I have endured. This time will be no different.

I am learning that it is okay to not be strong all the time. It's okay to have a bad day, be a couch bum, and stay in my pajamas all day. Sometimes it's needed. Needed as a time to refocus or reboot. Needed as a time to see how far I've come.

I am learning that it is awesome to be able to stand up for myself. No longer will I allow someone to walk all over me as if I have no brain or incapable of making my own decisions.

I am learning to use this period of time as a growing time. Struggle but win. Take life one day at a time. True friends are by my side.

You never know when your life will end or how much time you have left. Love those around you. Live in the moment of each breath you have. Stay focused on your dreams and goals. Keep learning and never give up!

-BonniferWW

When you've been at a job you love for several years, while working in small town America with people that you have grown to love, it becomes seriously difficult to think about leaving it all. It did for me. I'm the type that puts my heart and soul into that kind of job. I love my patients and care about what happens to them. I love the small town feel and atmosphere. I get emotionally attached to wherever I'm at and sometimes it's difficult to leave. Not always, just sometimes. This was one of those times.

When the county took over the ambulance service, I gave it a little time before I began looking for another job. I was very skeptical and didn't give it much hope. This was mostly because of who the county had chosen to run the service. She had a long history behind her of extremely poor management and running things into the ground.

I gave it a few months to discover that my gut had been correct. I quietly began job hunting. There was nothing much in the state of Indiana because here, you either had to also be a firefighter to go far or be satisfied doing transfers for forever. I had no interest in the fire side and I wanted more than transfers. I needed more.

I'm going to let you in on a little secret. I'm afraid of fire. I know....it is no longer a little secret. I can light a match and be fine. I can light a candle and be fine. I can light a bonfire and be fine. But expect me to walk inside a burning building, even with all the protective gear in the world? Nope, nope, and nope. No thanks. Absolutely no desire. Never have and never will. So yes, I always wear cute pajamas to bed in case of a house fire.... never know which fireman will have to help me to the door and outside. Ha-ha!

I began looking pretty much all over the country. At this point, I was willing to go anywhere that accepted the National Registry license. Most states do. A few states don't and require you to take their own qualifying test. My thinking is that I worked too hard for my National Registry to not use it. So if a state doesn't want to accept it, then I don't need to be in that state.

I applied for jobs in North and South Carolina, Kansas, Oklahoma, and I forget where else. I had a few interviews too, but never heard back. But then the recruiter from a Tulsa ambulance service called me. We scheduled a time for an interview. It would be my very first time in Oklahoma. I was both scared and excited. I kept it hush hush and told only a few people about my trip.

The weekend before the week of my interview, I began thinking too much as I commonly do. I began having thoughts like "What the hell am I thinking? I don't have money to move." or "How am I going to afford this?" or "I know I have to get out of Indiana or at least out of this job, but how with little money?" I emailed the recruiter and told him thanks but no thanks. The next Monday morning, he called me first thing and asked me what was up and what he could do to help. So I told him. I said that I couldn't afford the move and that I didn't know how I'd come up with the deposit and first month's rent if I got the job. He calmly told me to not worry about that. He said that on top of the sign on bonus, they had a relocation assistance program, too. He said they would help, but first the interview. I was to save all my receipts on the trip out for the interview and I'd be reimbursed if I were offered a job. Totally awesome!

Apparently, it was meant for me to at least go out for the interview. I loaded up the car and went with no clue what I was getting myself into or what the future may hold. I even enjoyed the drive out. It was almost freeing.... like letting a bird out of its cage. I felt like I was finally being able to see the world. I had been stuck in Indiana for so long. I felt like I was stuck in a rut and couldn't get out or that people wouldn't let me out. Maybe it was because they had a certain expectation of me and wouldn't let me do more. That's what I felt like anyhow, whether it was true or not. Some did try to tell me what I should or shouldn't do and I had to break off those relationships. If I didn't do what they "suggested", they would be upset. It was ridiculous and I just couldn't do it anymore. I was growing up FINALLY. That trip made me realize so much.

I arrived in Oklahoma and went to my interview. It was with several people at once, but they were very welcoming and friendly. It did amaze me how friendly people were in Oklahoma... so unlike Indiana. I remember being asked one medical question I couldn't remember the answer to. "What is a dystonic reaction and how do you treat it?" I debated to try to wing an answer or to be honest about not remembering it. I decided to be honest and said I didn't remember. They told me it was okay and that it would be covered in the academy. The rest of the interview went well. My recruiter had been in there with me. Afterwards, he walked me out and told me that I had rocked it. He said that I would hear within a few days. Well, it was later that afternoon when he called to offer me the job. I was kind of shocked really after being denied in all the other interviews, but oh so excited, too. I was going to be a paramedic at one of the top ambulance services in the country.

The next day, I went apartment hunting. The first place I went felt completely like home and they could also have a spot ready within two weeks for me. Why two weeks? Because I had two weeks to go home, pack up all my things, and be back in Tulsa ready to start in the next paramedic class. HOLY CRAP! What was I thinking?!?!?! Ha-ha! This was so awesome!.

I arrived home and told the world. I went and turned my resignation in to Beatrice which was a super celebration to me. I had to tell my landlords who were very understanding due to the circumstances. It seemed though that when I told anyone else, they just stood there in disbelief. Did they not believe me? Did they really think I didn't have the guts to think on my own? Did they seriously think of me in such fashion that I didn't have what it would take to venture out on my own to where I knew no one? Humph! I sure did and I would show them. Not to prove it to them or anything, but to prove it to myself that I was that strong and capable a woman. I didn't need to be dependent on others....in fact I was independent.

I packed up my car. If it didn't fit in my car, then it didn't go. I either sold it, gave it away, or trashed it. I attended a goodbye party. The night before my departure, a few friends and I went out for supper. Up until this point in my life, this was going to be one of the most difficult, most growing, and most exciting things I had ever done in my life. It truly ended up being one of the best decisions I have ever made in my life.

Chapter 13

The Tulsa Ambulance Service

What if

What if your life went the way you chose?

What if your life went only down the path of good?

What if your life went exactly as planned?

What if your life was roses and unicorns?

What if your life never had anything tragic?

What if your life never had any death?

What if your life never had to face any fears?

What if your life never had any uncertainty?

What if people close to you never meant you any harm?

What if people around you never were dishonest?

What if people around you never lived second lives?

What if people close to you weren't out seeking attention?

What if you could go back and change a move?

What if you could go back and change a decision?

What if you could go back and change a job choice?

What if you could go back and change a partner?

Would you?

Could you?

Might you?

If you hadn't gone through the fire, you wouldn't have discovered how strong you are.

If you hadn't gone through the fire, you wouldn't have discovered how beautiful you are.

If you hadn't gone through the fire, you wouldn't have discovered who your true friends are.

If you hadn't gone through the fire, you wouldn't have discovered how strongly you are loved.

If you hadn't gone through the fire, you wouldn't have found your biggest purpose in life.

If you hadn't gone through the fire, you wouldn't have found your new running buddies.

If you hadn't gone through the fire, You wouldn't have found your strong voice.

If you hadn't gone through the fire, you wouldn't have found your writing ability.

If you hadn't gone through the fire, you wouldn't have grown your friendships.

If you hadn't gone through the fire, you wouldn't have grown nearly as much spine.

If you hadn't gone through the fire, you wouldn't have grown in your sense of humor.

If you hadn't gone through the fire, you wouldn't have grown in your tenacity.

-BonniferWW

I left Indiana that early morning with tears in my eyes, but joy and peace in my heart knowing that I was heading to where I belonged. Tears of sadness that I was leaving what and who I knew, but also of joy that I was finally leaving what at times had seemed like a prison I couldn't escape. I was so ready to escape Indiana. It held far too many ugly memories and it was a way to let them all go. I made it in one day's drive and spent the night in a hotel as it was too late in the day to sign my lease.

My appointment wasn't until the early afternoon. So I slept in and hung out in the room for a while. But I was too excited to stay still for long, so I loaded up and found a place to do some shopping. Since I left almost everything behind, I was going to need plenty of things. But on the other hand, my car was so full, I couldn't buy very much until I got my car unloaded. I bought some little things such as a shower curtain and a toilet brush.

Finally I couldn't stand it anymore. The excitement was overflowing. I still had a couple hours before my appointment for the lease, but I didn't know what else to shop for that there was room for in my car. So I called and asked if I could come early. They said it was fine, but the carpet was still a bit damp. I seriously didn't care at that point. The Tulsa ambulance service had given me a check for my deposit and first month's rent so I was ready.

With my lease signed, now it was time to unload my car. It was literally 118 degrees outside, and my apartment was on the second floor. I had never lived in 118-degree weather before. If Indiana hit 100, people thought they were dying. I knew I wasn't dying of course, but I did wonder what in the world I was getting myself into AGAIN. It was rough, but I was glad I didn't have anything big and heavy to carry up there by myself. That really would have been rough.

The paramedic classes started Monday, so I only had a couple days to get settled. There were more shopping trips. I had to buy a bed and furniture too. Clothes hangers, food, toilet paper, etc. For the moment, I was too busy to have a moment for everything to sink in. I knew it would come though.

Here it was.... finally! The first day on the new job. The first day of the academy. Almost felt like I was a kid going back to school or something. I wasn't the only new out of state person, which was comforting, but I was probably the only out of state new female who had any dignity. The other female was very quickly being chased by the guys in the class. It was funny to watch......she was itty bitty in size too - probably a size zero.

I felt welcomed. I did get frustrated though because we had a quiz over a random topic every day. Such as the first time the instructor said to list all the highways in Tulsa. It was the second day of academy. There was no list of highways in our notebooks. None! I knew a few just from my 2 days of driving around. How was I supposed to list off the highways when you didn't give me a list to memorize? So when they would be read off for grading, that is when I copied them down and made my list. I may have or may have not gotten seriously worked up over this matter. Nerves, it was new job nerves though. Highways are on the map of course.

Classes were four weeks long and full of learning the protocol, equipment, directional, mapping, and so much more. Then there were all the drills, memorization, and testing to be able to begin my orientation rides on the ambulance. Once the rides were completed and my FTO (Field Training Officer) cleared me to be on my own, then I would find out what shift I was on and who my EMT would be.

I was so nervous about who my FTO would be. I was scared it would be some para-God, hot-tempered, rude person. Or someone that wouldn't work well with someone coming from out of state, especially several states away. This was a bit of a culture shock for me. Just a little.

My FTO was great and patient. I did five weeks of orientation rides. He kept me longer on orientation because of directional and learning the area, but otherwise things went great overall. He told me later that in the beginning he had questioned whether or not I'd survive "the big city of Tulsa" and the ambulance service. I told him that I had no choice. It was do or die.

I settled into things at work. I really enjoyed this even though I ran my tush off every shift. I actually had four partners for my first shift. All four were in paramedic school and were also doing clinicals. Their work schedules were based around class and clinicals. So I worked with them on off-school days. I loved having the variety and the fresh outlook plus it kept me on my toes. We all worked great together.

Not all partners work out that fabulous though. Every workplace has their characters who suck up to management but are despised by those who have to work with them. Of course, if you have the same attitude toward management, then you work great together, but otherwise not so much. I had an EMT named Amy. She was the type to suck up to management. Some saw right through her while others fell for her actions and words. She was a very loud person and everything she did had to be noticed. She also loved to text and drive. Yes, text while driving the ambulance. It didn't matter if we were driving lights and sirens to a call, driving to the hospital with a patient on board, or driving around town between calls.

That girl was glued to her phone. Company policy was no texting while driving. I had tolerated all I could take. I had been hesitant to say anything because I knew she would blow. One morning, we received a call first thing out of the gate. She was already texting and driving while responding to this call. I asked her nicely to please stop texting and driving. OH SHE WAS PISSED!

We arrived on scene and took care of our patient. Once we had the patient loaded and I was also in the back, Amy disappeared. As in I thought we were ready to transport and she was nowhere to be found. I waited. Nothing. I stuck my head outside to overhear her conversation on the phone. She was talking to the supervisor. What? Okay whatever.

After we cleared, we were told to head to corporate to see the supervisor. Great! Now I knew my wonderful partner had pulled something. We walked in and shut the door. He proceeded to tell me how I had refused to help Amy with directional and how it's my job as a paramedic to assist with directional. He went on and on. I tried to get a word in to tell him the truth, but I was ignored. I finally made him hear me that she had been texting and driving. He let it fall on deaf ears and began talking just as if I had said nothing. He also threatened me with write ups if our partner issues continued. She continued to text and drive, but only when I was in the back with patients. I continued to document and even took photos. I also discovered that she was spreading rumors that I didn't do anything on scene. I would just stand there if a patient began to get a little uptight or rambunctious. Uh okay. I knew my reputation was held high there and I knew I was well respected there at least among upper management, the education department, and the paramedics who mattered. Now opinion doesn't matter to an extent, but I wanted to do a decent job here. If Amy had stopped texting when I had asked her to, then things would have been fine.

I went on to grow to be a great paramedic. There was always something new to learn and something to improve upon. There were regular education requirements and meetings held. High standards were expected to be met. This place was exactly what I had needed to be able to flourish as a paramedic.

Speaking of mistakes, I made a huge one. Now during academy, education preaches how important capnography is. They preach how important the Medical Director believes in it. In fact, it is so highly important, that if you go more than 60 seconds without it attached to the ET tube on an intubated patient, it can get you a 30-day suspension in your paramedic license.

Well, I was working a ton of overtime trying to pay for my wedding. As in if the ambulance service was offering a bonus, (they always were at this point), then I was working. I was working far more than I was sleeping and I sure wasn't taking time any time for myself.

It happened. The unthinkable inevitable happened. I messed up. Now this patient was already intubated and was stable. In this instance, no harm was caused to the patient. My EMT and I were transporting from one hospital to another. We loaded the patient into the ambulance and began transport. The whole time my gut was telling me that I forgot something. As hard as I tried, I couldn't think of it. OH CRAP! I was in big trouble. My EMT that day was one I had never worked with before. He was in paramedic school but never said a word. Just stood there. This wasn't technically his fault though.

We arrived at the hospital and took care of the patient. I didn't know who the supervisor was that day, but I was sure praying it was someone with a heart and sympathy. I told my EMT what happened and that I was going to call the supervisor. Sure enough - the supervisor did have a heart. I was pulled off the truck for the rest of the shift. I had to fill out a bunch of paperwork, too.

Now it was waiting with dread the rest of the weekend for Monday to meet with the Medical Director. DREAD! The director himself was out of the office. So I had to meet with his staff which I think was almost worse. I had to do some remediation which consisted of a couple videos. Then of course the 30 days. I was allowed to work as an EMT though and was paid at my paramedic pay rate. I could have worked overtime too, but to me it was a sign that I desperately needed to slow down. If I kept going the way I was and I could have killed someone.

On my days off, I took my days off. I rested from work. I slept. I relaxed…. even if I was doing things that needed attending to. It was life away from work. You only have one life. Work is not everything. Don't make work your life. You will miss so much if you do that.

My contract at the ambulance service was for two years. I seriously considered staying. But they were going to be going through some drastic changes; taking away a $3 an hour raise they had just given everyone, requiring more work hours for the same annual wage, and more. I watched and talked to the long-time veterans. I waited. When things became certain, I knew my time was done and turned in my two-week notice.

Another heavy day for it was my last day at the ambulance service. I had a new job waiting for me, but this employer had moved me out here. If it hadn't been for them, I may still be stuck in Indiana. You never know where difficult roads may lead you. Don't ever be afraid to take them.

Chapter 14

My Dream of Running

Two Brothers

Running.

I used to hate you,

But that was before I met you.

I used to despise you,

But that was before I knew you.

Running,

That one day, running a 5k,

You forever changed my life.

I didn't realize that little start line

Could be so life changing.

Running,

You've carried me through

Some rather dark days.

You pushed me to go farther

Then I thought I could possibly go.

Running,

You've saved my life

More than a couple times.

You've cleared my head

Too many times to count.

Running,

I never knew how much I needed you

Until I didn't have you.

I didn't realize how much you were a part of me

Until we were no longer allowed together.

But then dear Running,

I met your brother Walking.

While we may be separated for a short while,

We will be reunited soon to run again.

So Walking,

I must say you have had to teach me patience

These last few years…..and maybe the next 10.

You have taught me to slow down

To enjoy nature around me while walking.

Walking,

We also have had many victories and struggles,

Crossing finish lines and crossing off states.

Walking neighborhood circles for a virtual half marathon

And having many walking conversations with friends.

Walking,

You've watched as I've shed many a tear,

You've seen me as I cuss like a sailor in frustration,

You've seen me with no fight left in my sails.

You've seen me with nothing left to give.

Then it comes.

Walking,

As you and Running both know,

It is at that exact moment,

That the strength rushes in.

It is at that exact moment,

That the fight is back on.

It is at that exact moment,

That I know I will finish this race.

It is at that exact moment,

That the fear is gone.

It is at that exact moment,

That the tenacity is back in full swing.

It is at that exact moment,

That i know I can do this.

It is that exact moment when the world knows to stay out of the way. For they know that as long as I am walking or running, they had best be on their toes. And when the time comes that i can no longer run or walk, there will still be a way to get my racing in. I will just figure it out when I get there.

-BonniferWW

Do you have a dream? Are you a dreamer? Big dreams? Small dreams? Of course you are. I am too. We all have dreams right. Many of us go after them and accomplish them. Maybe some just sit by and not. But those who do see how big the world is and how much they can accomplish and so much more.

As a young child, I had a big dream. I told my mother once what it was, and she laughed in my face. That response was not surprising giving that's the way they were about everything. That dream was running. Oh how I dreamed of running a race. It didn't matter what or where. Of course, then I knew nothing of local races or that sort of thing or of even the Chicago or Boston Marathons. But I knew about the Olympics. When it came time for the running events, I was glued to the TV……when I was allowed anyhow. If Mom and Dad left the house for whatever reason, I turned the TV on to see if any running events were on. I knew I'd probably never run in the Olympics, but also knew there had to be other running events somewhere somehow that I could participate in.

I NEVER TOLD ANYONE OF MY DREAM AGAIN.

Life went on. I still seriously intently watched the Olympic running events through the years growing up. There was no internet back then. We were kept so secluded and under control that I knew nothing of local races or that they even existed. I knew no other way of getting involved in anything running. I thought my dream was lost.

Still, I kept it buried. Still, it was there. Still, it ached inside me. Time went by. School had no such thing as Cross country or Track or any sports as such. They barely had anything really. I was in high school when they finally started a volleyball team for the girls. That was the only sport they had for us girls. Then that was a popularity contest to get on the team. So I was definitely out on that one.

I grew up. I went to college. They had a cross country team for girls, but I was too shy to try out especially with no previous training or experience. In my mind, there was no possible way I'd make the team in my shape. I didn't even try. I didn't even go talk to the coach. Nothing. I possibly could have started my dream then. Who knows right? It sucked being so extremely shy then. Oh it was horrible. Anyway, it's all water under the bridge as they say. Still I wonder. Oh well.

After college, I moved out of the house. Still I kept my dream buried. I probably even forgot about it at this point. Like I'm in my late 20's. How can I start running now? Or I'm too fat? (I was a bit chubby.) People don't start running this late in life. If you see me running, you better run too. Ha-ha! You know the comments. But still the ache was there, I knew it was. I could feel it even if it was subconsciously.

Then the move to Oklahoma happened. (See Chapter 12) I was working at the Tulsa ambulance service and my partner at the time was Rachel. She and I had some crazy times together. Some days we could be great friends. Other days we could absolutely despise each other. But we did work great together on calls. We knew what the other was going to do and synced well. While we'd be sitting in the ambulance posting waiting for the next call, she'd usually be knitting, and I'd be crocheting.

One day, while doing our thing sitting in the truck, she asked me if I'd do a 5k race with her. At first, I just laughed at her. I had the usual response that we already talked about. You know, the comments and all. But it had struck a nerve. It hit hard. This was my chance. A 5k race! I could run a race with a friend and not alone. I'd be fulfilling my dream FINALLY! Who knows what could happen next?

I changed my laughter to a yes. Rachel wanted to do the Sweetheart run put on by Fleet Feet. The money would go to a charity that helped various shelters. We researched how to train for a 5k and decided to train with the couch potato to a 5k program. We planned out our training schedule and agreed we were going to run on the Riverside trail.

The planning was great, but executing the plan was horrible. I think I can count on one hand the number of times we went running. Whoops. Rachel has horrible asthma, and she had a rough time with running. Eventually she decided she was going to drop out. Me? I was already too far in and too excited to quit. Additionally, it was too close to race day. I had bought my outfit too, which by the way, was more for an early fall race or a fast runner. This race was mid-February.

The closer it got to race day, the more nervous I became. I was scared. What if I couldn't keep up? What if I was the last one to cross the finish line? Is it okay to walk in a race? What if I couldn't finish? What do you do if you get hurt? What if I get lost and miss a turn? All these questions and so many more. I kept posting them on Facebook and asking a couple of running friends. A couple experienced family members on Facebook assured me I was okay and would be fine on race day, but still........ Friends I asked in person ended up not having a clue but tried to pretend they did. They were trying to be helpful and assuring though. I do have to give them credit for that.

Race day finally arrived. My dream was here! I felt like I could seriously vomit. I was so crazy, excited, and nervous. Rachel and Charley were both there to support me. I had told Rachel that if she was backing out running with me, that she had better be there to support me since it was her fault I was doing this. She was a good friend and showed up.

We lined up in the starting corral. I was freezing cold. It was 28 degrees that early morning. Races always start so early in the morning. I was in the back half of the pack. The starting gun went off and we were all on our way. The first mile was rough. I couldn't breathe. Oh the nerves. The need to vomit. The excitement. I was holding back tears of joy. But I was doing it. I was running. I was living my dream! Oh yes!

Mile 2 was easier. I fell into a pace. The nerves calmed down a bit. I warmed up. My fingers were still frozen though, but oh well. I knew I had this. I had people around me, encouraging me. Complete strangers chatting with others they didn't know from Adam. It was unbelievable. Everyone was so friendly. I began to feel as if my worries were unnecessary. The being last or unable to walk or getting lost or whatever.

Mile 3 was happening. I was almost finished. I was almost to the finish line. I was beginning to hear the announcer and the cheering of the crowd. I had begun getting tired after two miles, but somehow hearing the crowd and knowing I was almost finished gave me energy, motivation, and the 'umph' to run faster. The adrenaline flowed. I almost couldn't breathe because of it. I rounded the last few turns. The roar of the announcer and crowd became louder. It wasn't for me, but I pretended it was. I knew I had two people in the crowd cheering for me. I went for the last turn and then saw the huge inflatable sign that said, "FINISH LINE". Inwardly I gulped with tears and excitement. My eyes filled with tears of joy. I ran as hard as I could muster. I don't know If I can explain the emotions that filled me as I crossed that finish line, but it was like nothing I've ever experienced. EVER! Even now, with all the races I've done, this one still stands out as the biggest and probably one of the two most emotional races I've completed. I'll tell you about the second in a bit. The emotions that filled me were unbelievable. I had worked hard toward, had lived and fulfilled my dream of running. After years and years of keeping it hidden and buried, I had finally accomplished it. You know y'all, you can, too - no matter what it is. Go live your dreams. I don't care what it is. Get out there and do it. Life is far too short to not.

After crossing that finish line, I was hooked. I went looking for the next race and the next one. I did several 5k's. My confidence grew. My running improved greatly. I began to realize how much running was helping, not just physically but also mentally, spiritually, and emotionally, too. I was beginning to go through rough times in my marriage. Charley was drinking heavily. I began finding out things that I didn't want to know. But more about that in chapter 15 and 16. Running cleared my head and helped me to figure out what to do. It helped me to breathe emotionally if that makes sense.

After doing 5ks, I wanted more. I wanted a bigger challenge. So I went for 10ks (6.2 miles). I did a few of those, but decided it wasn't a big enough challenge. If I can do a 10k, then I can do a half marathon right. A half marathon is 13.1 miles. Pfffffft. That's not that bad.

A half marathon you say? Oh, was I wrong. I thought for sure I was going to die. I thought it would never end. My first half was the Route 66 Marathon in Tulsa, Oklahoma. It is a doozy with all the hills. They do make it fun though by having music along the way and different themes at the water stops. People in different neighborhoods come out to cheer on the runners, too. It's amazing how much strangers cheering you on can give you energy to continue. Runners around me would find out it was my first and they would be extra encouraging. Completely incredible!

I thought I'd never reach even Mile 10, but I surely did. Then I told myself that I only had a 5k left. Anyone can run a 5k right? Except me who's in the middle of dying at Mile 10. "Stop being so dramatic," I told myself. I did hurt what seemed like badly at the time. Everything ached - upper body down to my toes. I could feel blisters on my feet. I don't remember if I had Brooks shoes then or not but it did take me awhile to find a decent pair of running shoes.

Finally, I made it to Mile 13 - 1.1 miles left. In the moment, I decided this was awesome and I knew I'd finish, but I would NEVER do another half marathon again. It hurt too much. It was too long. People are crazy for doing this long of a race. It took me way too much time to complete it. I realized how slow a runner I am. Blah blah blah.

Then there was the finish line. I felt like I floated across the finish line. Floated as in adrenaline and excitement and oh holy crap! I just did a HALF MARATHON! I couldn't believe it. My medal was placed around my neck. I had to keep looking at it to make sure. Was this a dream? Nope, no dream. Completely real baby. Your dream just became bigger. I know I said I'd never do another half marathon, but well, two days later, I was back on the computer looking for the next half. I couldn't help myself. It was like an addiction. I was on cloud nine and I needed more of this. Yes, I still hurt a bit and the memories of the severe pain and blisters were drifting from memory.

When you're learning about running or new to running, it's amazing the things you learn to do that you never thought you would need in life. Things like needing to spit, but not just spit. You have to aim your spit so that you don't hit other runners. You learn how to pee behind a bush, or behind a rock, or in the woods. Yes, for real. I'm serious. And you learn to do it quickly. Doesn't matter if it's dead of winter either. Running will make your bladder decide it needs to go NOW when you are five miles from home and you are two miles from town. Pee woman! Running also teaches you how to choose a proper fit shoe. Yes, you really do need to go be fitted professionally at a shoe store. I don't mean just on that weird metal looking thing that you slide your foot on either. It involves walking on a treadmill, having the associate video your walking to see how you walk, and then trying on several pairs of shoes to see what you like. How you walk decides what type of shoe you need. But don't ask me all those questions because I'm not a professional shoe fitter.

Anyhow, I went through many many types of shoes before I found Brooks. No, I'm not advertising for Brooks. I'm just sharing my story here. You have to wear the shoe that is best for you. My first pair of running shoes were not Brooks. I wore them for a 5k. Let's just say that way before I finished, I could feel a ginormous blister forming. By ginormous I mean bigger than a half dollar. Yuck! Yes, I popped it when I got home. Ewww. Enough said.

I continued doing half marathons and it became my favorite distance. Why? It was long enough to push you hard, but not enough to make you die. But eventually, you guessed it, I needed another big challenge. If I can do a half marathon, why not go for a full marathon. Hehe.

My first full marathon was also the Route 66 Marathon in Tulsa. Why that one? Because it was the only one I could find where they make a big deal about it being your first full marathon. It should be a big deal. Your medal and your bib both stated that it was your first marathon. I trained hard I thought. I did skip days of training though to be honest. Again, I had no clue what I was getting myself into. It's some seriously hot training in the sun in order to run a marathon in the late fall. Whew! But it got done.

On race day, I felt like it may as well have been my very first race. I was so nervous and scared spitless. I had all the same questions then that I had way back at that very first 5k. My stomach was all nerves. I couldn't breathe. I felt like I could puke. I knew I hadn't trained enough. But then, how do you know if you have trained enough for a full marathon?

Well, the gun sounded, and we were off. In this big of a race, the first few miles are quite crowded. So it's difficult to run much or very fast. Eventually people spread out and runners can settle into their individual paces. I tried to focus on each mile I was in and not think about the fact that I had to do a whole whopping 26 freaking miles. Like what the what was I thinking and I'm only in mile 4. Right!?!?

We settled in. People around me noticed my bib that it was my first marathon and cheered me on extra. Runners and spectators alike cheered me on. It greatly helped to know that people were there for me even as complete strangers. We neared Mile 8 which is known as the "party mile" and you know what that means? Alcohol! In this case, it meant jello shots and lots of them. Boy were they delicious and refreshing.

The miles trudged on. 10.....12..... Then at about 12 and a half miles, the half participants and full participants split. It's seriously rough though because at the split, you can hear the finish line. It's less than a mile. As a full marathoner, it's seriously tempting to call it a day and go with that half. But no, I didn't, and don't know the meaning of the word "quit". So I kept on. Shortly after I turned the corner, I met this other runner. At the time, I thought she was an angel because I had thought of quitting due to the pain even though I seriously wanted to do this. She saw it was my first full and stepped right in pace with me. She kept me moving, got my pace up. She told me something that has stayed with me to this day, "If you can move your hips and you can move your knees, then you are fine. Keeping going." She was surely right. She said she'd stay with me for a while. The time went by along with the miles. The pain didn't seem so bad.

We hit the dreaded Mile 20. I had never been at Mile 20 before. I cried. Then Mile 21. I cried a lot. I didn't care who was around me. I had hit the wall. I felt like I literally could not go any longer. This friend verbally picked me up and kept me going. Spectators cheered us on. Music played loudly. Miles 22, 23, 24. "Maybe I'd actually make it", I thought to myself. The worst is over. There's only two miles left. I've come all this way. You know there's no quitting or dying or getting hurt now. Somewhere along the line, my new angel friend had disappeared, and I never saw her again. I was going to hug her and tell her thank you again at the finish line, but oh well.

I continued on. Mile 25, 26. Jiminy Crickets! I'm in Mile 26. (Yes, other words were used to describe my excitement which I choose not to use here at the moment.) I turned the last corner. It had taken me over eight hours to complete. There was no crowd, no announcer, no one I knew to welcome me across the finish line. But it didn't matter at that moment. I saw that huge 'FINISH LINE' marker three blocks away. I sure hoped the photographer was there. I saw him as I got closer.

Suddenly the pain was gone. It was like running on air. Nothing else mattered. It was me and that finish line. I stared at it. It was all mine. I crossed it and yes, I was in tears. Happy tears. I had really done it! A full marathon! You know how many people actually complete a full marathon? According to Google, it's 0.5%. That is worldwide, not just nationally. That makes it even more of a big deal. It's huge!

I could barely walk. We won't talk about stopping to sit down and then trying to stand to walk again. Ha! That's far worse than Mile 20. But a friend showed up to take me home with a small detour to Hideaway Pizza. My motto is always eat pizza after a half or full marathon. Why? Because you've burned off so many calories you're going to be craving those carbs anyway until you eat them. So may as well go big and eat them right off. After my next marathon, which I'll tell you about in just a minute, I went with a group of friends to this fancy restaurant, I think it was Chinese. But it was the type that served fancy food, but not much of it.... if you know what I mean. This was the first real meal too afterwards. All we had had were snacks up to this point. I was still hungry and greatly craving pizza. I had spent enough money to have paid for four or five meals at a fast-food place. I hadn't cared because it was a marathon celebration. Anyway, I left Chicago to drive back home to Oklahoma the next day with planning to stop halfway because of hurting so bad and knowing my feet would swell. By the time I did stop for the night, I was so hungry for pizza and craving carbs so badly, I thought something was incredibly wrong with me. Well, there was…. it's called hunger. When I checked into my hotel room, I immediately ordered a pizza. I asked if the delivery guy could please bring it to my room even though they normally met up in the lobby since I had just run a full marathon. There was a chuckle on the line and then a yes. Thank you! The pizza arrived and I gave the guy a huge tip. I didn't even care how big. I just needed this pizza. I ate over half of a large pizza all by myself. It would be completely embarrassing except for the fact of just finishing a marathon. I felt so much better afterwards - it was amazing.

Now that I got ahead of myself, let's back up a second. After my first half marathon, and realizing how out of shape I was, and that I probably needed a wee bit of help, I went in search of a personal trainer. I had never really had a personal trainer before although I had seen them at work. They tell their client what to do and how many. Then the trainer stands there with a clipboard in hand, with a seriously bored look on their face, looking around for a hot chick/dude to stare at, all while being a "personal trainer". Right! Well, I signed up at Gym A and received a couple sessions with a trainer. Great! Yeah, it was a dud. Ended up not liking the gym much either. Went to Gym B and then Gym C. Same thing. There were good and bad points of each but still. I don't think I'm that picky. I just expect things like equipment to work or locks on bathroom doors to work or employees to look like they half enjoy their job. Maybe a trainer who would actually kick your booty hard……. who you would not dare to utter the words "What else have you got?". Not asking a lot.

Well, my wish was about to happen. This guy contacted me online about coming to workout at his gym at downtown Tulsa. At first I was like what? I've never heard of that guy or the gym before. I was so nervous to go down there and start. He looked like this big muscled guy and like he could pick your butt up and toss you 500 feet. Now, he didn't have the mean look at all. His eyes spoke of anything but evil. Like without his face, you'd think he might actually throw your butt 500 feet if you messed up. He'll have some smartass comment here I'm sure. Anyhow, finally, I went down to meet him and sign up. His name is Johnny. Little did I know how much this guy would change my life and also be a part in helping to save my life.

Johnny would learn someone quickly. Then he'd push them hard and a little more the next session. If you were expecting the typical trainer here, then you may as well go back home to bed. Here? You'd better come in with your A game. He knew if you weren't doing your best. He always knew that crap. Always! There wasn't a day I left that gym that I wasn't soaked with sweat. Obviously, some days more than others. Johnny would push and push hard but he also truly cares about his clients. Work, school, home. Everything.

There were many days that I would get irritated, frustrated, and sometimes even angry at him. But he kept pushing me hard to be the best version of me. It wasn't just at the gym either. He was having some vehicle issues, so I began helping him with rides and such. We had many conversations about life and my background and how I can become a better person. He always made me think and see things in a different light. Things made sense when he explained them.

I was in the best shape of my life now. This was awesome and I felt great. Johnny had worked with me for over a year to help me get ready for the Chicago Marathon. The registration for this race is done lottery style. I put in for it thinking there is no way because this is one of the top five world marathons. Well, I got in. So Johnny worked my butt into shape. I seriously thought I was going to die. He said his goal was to make me vomit. So I told him to just not call the EMS service in Tulsa, Oklahoma. I really didn't want to take over eight hours again to run a full.

Chicago Marathon time came. I went with a small group of girlfriends. By the way, in the world of running, it's amazing how many people I've met and how many of those I've met have become great friends. I met Polly and Elina through a Facebook running singles group and now we've run several races together over the last few years. So anyhow, (Squirrel!) I had never gotten to see the side of Chicago like I was about to get to see. From the subway stations to the constant people, to the driving skills of the Uber driver. I was the only one in our little group to do the 5k, but Polly came with me and met me at the finish line. During the race, per my GPS, I was running approximately a 10 to 11-minute-mile pace. I was like 'what-the-what' because I never go that fast. Turned out that the GPS was getting messed up with all of the tall buildings.

Race day came. Full marathon number two was about to start. I was a tad more confident about this one. I had trained hard for it. Plus Johnny was going to track me on the race app and help me keep my speed up.

The start gun went off. The individual corrals started. Of course it was a while before we went. But the crowd by the start line was big and loud. Way to wake up early Chicago! This race was the biggest race I'd done so far. The welcome was huge. The city was huge. The number of runners was huge. Incredible! It was kind of like a first race, but not really because obviously this was so different. The nerves and excitement were similar though.

I was across the start line. At first, it felt almost impossible to run decent because of how crowded it was. I grew frustrated because I had a goal to meet. I wanted to be under six hours and in my mind, this was far from a good start. But I told myself to chill out because it would get better.

The first miles began to pass. Yes, the crowd did span out a bit and I did calm down and get to speed up. Of course. I tried to remember to look around me and enjoy the scenery because it seemed I tended to forget to do that often. After the race, other runners would be talking about scenery or an animal they saw or a cool building or whatever and I would have totally missed it. I might have been completely focused on my race time or lost in my music and thoughts or trying to pass another set of runners that I completely missed most everything around me. Focus on the mile you're in is what I attempted to remember.

By this time, I was nearing the middle miles. My trainer had texted me my mile time. I was also beginning to cramp which isn't good this early on, but one of the water stops had pretzels. I grabbed a handful along with two glasses of Gatorade. It seemed to help.

I was nearing the later miles. My speed was slowing down. I was seriously struggling. Johnny was texting me more often now telling me to speed up. It was somewhere in the 20 something miles that I hurt so badly and was crying so hard, that I texted him to say that I never wanted to do this ever again. He told me to step it up and get moving. Ha! Just like him. No whining just shut up and do the mission in front of you.

At mile 23, I began giving myself a long chew out session which literally lasted a mile long. Remember those long talks from your parents as a kid that you dreaded or the family meetings or maybe even the sermons at church or the lectures in college. Yeah, all of those really. Only this was me talking to myself and myself had to pay attention to me talking or else. Oh I lectured hard. I told myself that I hadn't worked my ass off this whole last year plus to sluff off now, I hadn't worked my ass off to be lazy now, and I sure hadn't worked my ass off to wish later I had pushed myself harder now. By the end of the mile, I was ready for the lecture to end. Hehe.

At mile 24, I pulled up my shoestrings, and even though it hurt to high heaven, I began to run again. Of course, by this time, it could hardly be called a run. It was more of a sloth jog. But I did it. Mile 25. I was going to do it. I was going to do it AGAIN! Mile 26. Over another bridge and hearing the announcer and oh that crowd......I love that crowd. It lifts you right up. It carries you that last bit in a race straight to the finish line. 26.1 I could see that absolutely huge finish line. The crowd was going loudly. I knew I was going to be slightly over my goal, but at this point I didn't care. I was here....at the Finish Line. It was happening all over again! I keep saying that, but each race I do is so very special in its own way. Each race reminds me of my dream and how I got to where I am today. It reminds me of how I fought to overcome my fears of going out there to reach for my dream too.

I crossed the FINISH LINE! I had really done and did it. AND at a top 5 world marathon too! My time was 6:07:23. I had taken just under an hour off of my full marathon time. Oh yeah baby! That is huge! Marathon number 2 was in the books.

Now it's time for something immensely personal. Remember how I said I had been helping Johnny out giving him rides and stuff? Well, I had been doing it for awhile. There was that. I had let him borrow my car a couple times too while I was gone to work because of the length of my long shifts. Then he got lost every time coming to pick me up. I grew extremely frustrated. Okay okay, even mad. I never mentioned it to him. Never. So instead of mentioning it to him and talking to him about it, I disappeared. I blocked him. I stopped going to the gym. He had no clue what happened.

It was a long time before I even contacted him again. In fact, it wasn't even until after the incident had happened that I talked to him. I told him what had happened to me and why I suddenly wanted to talk and make things right. I told him what had upset me initially and why I had disappeared. We hashed it out - the differences, what should have happened, the way to handle it next time.

Now? I started going back to his gym again, that is until the pandemic hit. I had also tried to ride the bus down there and just couldn't do it on my own. Barry had ridden the bus with me one night. Then Lorna and I took the bus to the gym, walked the rest of the way just like I'd have to, walked back to the bus stop, and got on the bus. That was even difficult. Doing it alone made me ill. Maybe down the road I'll be able to do it alone. Time will tell.

Anyhow, all that to say that if you have a problem with someone or something doesn't sit right with someone, go talk to them. Tell them politely how you feel and what is wrong. Most likely, if you do it respectfully, they will be understanding at the very least. They will work with you and will work to a solution with you. I know Johnny and I would have no problems.

I've continued to do the Sweetheart Run every year because it's my running anniversary race. It's a very special race. Even after the incident, while lying in the hospital bed, one big thing I thought of was the Sweetheart run. I knew I had to be there at that starting line. I didn't care how I had to do it. The first time the neurosurgeon came in after I was extubated, I asked him when I could start training for my next marathon. He was completely speechless. It was great. After several seconds, he finally stated in a few months. That was too long for me and unacceptable. Big surprise there. I was too dizzy to even walk in the hospital. It took 2 people to help me to the bathroom. Physical therapy brought me a walker that had arm rests on it to help me walk better and on my own. That was all I needed. I began walking the halls. When visitors came, I'd ask them if they wanted to go walk with me. Some did and some didn't. Sometimes, I was too tired to. But around and around I went. I was determined to build up strength for that 5k.

Eventually, I went home from the hospital with Cleo and Patricia. Every day, when Patricia got home from work, we'd go in the garage and I'd walk circles around her car until I was too tired to continue. Slowly I was able to increase my walking minutes. Slowly I became a little stronger. Cleo told me I was absolutely not doing that 5k. Patricia said I could do that 5k. I told Cleo to shove it because I was doing that 5k and that Julie would see to it and sneak me out of the house if need be.

I had a checkup with my primary care physician. He himself was a former runner so he understood me. I told him what I wanted to do. He told me he would allow me to do the 5k as long as I abided by a few rules: 1. I used my walker. 2. I walked with friends. 3. Someone had a wheelchair available at all times along the route in case I couldn't complete it. There were a couple other rules too. Absolutely Doc! I could have hugged him right there. Cleo was with me and just gave me the stink eye.

Race day came. Julie picked me up. We were both so incredibly excited, like there are no words to describe this kind of excitement. When I'm supposed to be dead, but here I am, being allowed and getting to walk my anniversary race? Yeah, no words. So many friends walked with me that day. Amanda, Jullie, and Ashley especially. We followed doctor's orders to a T.

At the start line, I felt like my heart was pounding and my stomach was in my chest. This was big, like almost bigger than my first ever race. I couldn't breathe. The excitement was so huge. People looked at me and the walker as if questioning if I was even supposed to be there. Both hands were bandaged up from broken fingers. I had stitches and staples still in my head. I looked fabulous. I was quite the fashion statement. We found out later that several people had asked the race director if I was supposed to be there and okay to be walking in the race.

The race began. I and my race group were off. There were around 8 or 9 of us I think. I didn't pay much attention to miles on this race, but I did pay attention to each step. I wasn't supposed to be here and I wasn't supposed to be able to walk. It didn't matter to me that I couldn't run or that I had to use a walker or people's weird looks or that my time would be even more slow than before. Nothing of it mattered. It only mattered that I was there. It only mattered that my friends were there. It only mattered that we were all there in that exact moment at that race if that makes sense.

The miles went by. I walked by strangers. I walked quickly considering my shape and condition. Those around me kept asking me if I was doing okay. I was so exhausted, but there was no stopping me. I was not using that wheelchair until I crossed that finish line. I do not know the meaning of the word quit. Then there she was…...the finish line. Julie and I looked at each other. My eyes began to water. My innards were already bawling. We all headed straight for it. It was only a couple blocks away. No stopping us. We crossed it. Julie and I hugged each other. I began to shake, like those shakes your body does right before sobbing. Julie whispered in my ear, "Don't cry, don't cry". She knew that if I cried, she would also. Well, it was too late. I sobbed and so did she. Yes, this race was bigger than my first race. Sorry first race. This race meant so much more. Not only was it a reminder of where I had started from, but it was also a celebration of life. It was showing the world that everything is possible. A very evil man tried to take my dreams away from me. I showed him (even in his suicide) that I'm bigger and stronger than he ever was. I showed him that I don't quit. When things are horrible in life, when things are so dark, when things are the worst ever, please don't give in. Please find someone to talk to.

There have been several more races since, even a full marathon. The Cincinnati Flying Pig races, Little Rock Marathon, Hattiesburg Mississippi virtual half, and more. Julie vowed she'd never she would never do a full marathon. But she did when her little Wonder Woman Bonbon asked her to. We have done a couple half marathons together and several 5ks too. I was dubbed Wonder Woman while in the hospital and the name has stuck. So my outfit for races has become Wonder Woman. My walker is always decked out in Wonder Woman decor to match.

Every race is special to me. Each race has its own special memories. Each race also teaches me something about myself. Each race is a step closer to where I want to be. It's like a teaching moment almost every single time. It's being able to use my story, whether I have the opportunity to share it or not, to encourage others. People see me on my walker participating in a race and are encouraged or even chastised because they know if I can do it, then they should be out there doing it too. That's not being rude to me or downgrading or degrading or anything to me. It's just showing them that there are people who have it worse than them who are out there living life. If you can walk, talk, and live a normal life, don't take it for granted. If you can have kids, a family, and friends, don't take them for granted either. Everything can change in an instant. Everything can be taken from you. People will walk away from you when your life turns upside down. People will disappear when you need them the most. Those who do stick around are the ones who truly love and care about you. I've lost friends and family through this. Yes, it's rough, but you can either wallow in it or grow and make new friends. In times of hardship, you really do find out who your true friends are. Find someone who you can help and then help them. It will make your day 100 times better.

What's in a friend?

A friend can hug you,

Laugh with you,

Cry with you,

Sorrow with you,

Or triumph with you.

A friend can walk miles with you,

Participate in races with you,

Meet race milestones with you,

Conquer marathon miles along side you,

And share in those victories together.

A friend will stay up all night with you

Talking about nothing,

Talking about everything,

Talking about life's challenges,

Talking about life's victories,

And share in life's hilarities.

A friend will stop at nothing in their ability to help you,

In ironing yards upon yards of fabric for masks,

In cooking for the homeless,

In telling you what you need to hear,

In being a listening ear even on your crabby days,

In being your strength when you feel like you are weak,

in taking you in to help you all the more,

And to help in many ways more.

A friend is unbelievable.

A friend is fantastic.

A friend is real.

A friend is there.

A friend is crazy.

A friend is straightforward.

A friend is honest.

A friend is love.

A friend will cause "trouble" with you.

A friend will keep you from getting arrested.

A friend will be protective of you as necessary.

A friend will travel the unknown world with you.

A friend will always

Be there,

Love you for you,

Care for you,

Be honest to you,

And giggle with you.

Friends for life.

Friends forever.

-BonniferWW

Chapter 15

My marriage

The Dark

When the burden seems too heavy.....help someone else carry their struggles.

When it seems you can't take another step.....help someone else take two.

When it seems the grief is too much.....make someone else smile.

When the pain seems to be too great.....find strength in those who have chosen to be by your side.

When the darkness is at its darkest.....let a friend be your light.

When you feel lost far beyond ever being found.....take that outstretched hand.

For in your darkest your, you may still be someone else's brightest light.

In your darkest moment, you may give someone else strength to carry on.

You smile, your grace, your strength, your determination, your tenacity, your heart. It is in your darkest of dark moments where you see yourself for who you truly are, where you find what you are truly made of, and where you discover what you truly desire.

Almost every little girl dreams of the man she will one day marry. She dreams of her handsome prince on the giant white stead coming to take her to the palace where they will live happily ever after. Maybe not that mushy and romantic, but you get the idea. I'm sure guys are the same way whether they admit it or not. But each of us look forward to the person we will one day spend our lives with for the long-term. I was no different.

From the time I was a little girl, I imagined my prince being tall, strong, and handsome. He'd fight off the dragons, put out fires from the palace kitchen stove, and smash the ginormous spiders who dared enter the guarded walls. Hehe. Well, that is a good start, especially the protection from ginormous spiders.

During the whole process of moving, it did cross my mind if I would actually find someone out in Oklahoma. I'd daydream about what way I would stumble upon him. Would it be a car wreck and he would be a patient? Maybe he'd be a nurse or a doctor. Or maybe I'd meet him while I was eating by myself at a restaurant. The adventure of the unknown right?

Once I was settled in my apartment and job and once I began to feel like this new world was actually "home", I decided to sign up on Match.com. I know everyone has their personal opinions about dating online, but we're not here to discuss that. I am just going to say this though: please use your head about it, be smart, use safe calls. If something doesn't feel right, then it isn't. Trust your gut. Okay, end of the soap box moment. Anyway, back to Match. I scrolled through hundreds of profiles. Met a few guys. Nothing really stood out. This continued off and on for a while. Mostly first dates.

One day, somehow I had scheduled 2 dates in one day. That had never happened before. Like I was doing good to get one date. How in tarnation did I manage to get two? So I had a lunch date and then a dinner date.

The lunch date was rough. The guy struggled to hold a conversation. He waited for me to initiate everything and to ask all the questions. His way of asking me a question was to ask a question that I had just asked him. Every single time. Yep. The time dragged by. Finally lunch was over and I could escape. I did feel bad for the guy because I could tell he was intrigued by me and was interested, but I would never see him again.

The supper date was different. We met at Olive Garden. I could tell this guy, Charles, was definitely different.....at least much better than lunch dude different. We had a 45 minute wait for our table and so sat outside on a bench and chatted.

Oh that nervous giddy chatter that happens on the first date. He told me that he had had to cancel a first date the previous week. I was curious as to why he would cancel a date. Hmmm.....stomach ache? Family emergency? Got called into work? Too much acne? Sprained ankle? Nope, nope, and nope. He said that the girl had sent him a naked picture of herself. Now here's a guy with some decent character.

We got our table and continued talking through dinner. He seemed to relax some and I did too. He was really nice. Handsome too. For once, he didn't disappear to the restroom or play on his phone. Oh how it drives me nuts when the person you go on a date with has his nose stuck in the cell phone during the whole date. How are you supposed to have a decent conversation? You aren't really listening to the other person either if you're concentrating on your phone.

We finished supper, and said our goodbyes. He said he would call and text me later. I wasn't sure if I should believe him or not since so many guys say that, but then never do. Seems like it's a polite way of ending the evening or something.

He did text me. A lot. We talked often. We went out on more dates. A second date turned into more. Before you knew it, we were inseparable. We were always together when neither of us were working.

One day, I was at his house waiting for him to get home from work. He called me to tell me to go into the bathroom, close the door, and stay there until he got home and told me it was okay to come out. I was like uh okay sure.

He came home. I heard noise beyond the door as if he was setting something up or getting something ready. Then he hollered that I could come out. I opened the door. I saw him and he looked really nervous for some reason. I wondered if this was going to be the big moment I had been waiting for. You know, the moment when he proposes. By now, I was all the way in the living room. I saw the flowers, and the large bottle of wine. My gut told me this may just be that moment. Then I looked at Charlie. He looked a little pale, nervous, and excited. Then suddenly, there he was down on one knee. Holy crap! He was going to propose! He then asked me to marry him and be his wife forever. I said YES! He then put the ring on my finger and we kissed. We kissed like never before.

Oh how excited I was to live my life with my best friend. We were married July 12, 2014. We went on a Carribean cruise for our honeymoon. Oh how it was beautiful. Belize and a couple other stops. We even went swimming with the dolphins which had been a dream of mine.

We came home and settled into life. Our relationship was great.....for awhile. We never yelled at each other, never argued, and never fought. But things began to decline greatly.

While we were dating, I never saw him drink much. But now, he was almost constantly drunk on the weekends. Drunk to the point that I had to "babysit" him. Plus he had received a DUI about a mile from home one night. He started a bonfire because he wanted hot dogs, but literally almost fell into the fire. He'd vomit because of being so drunk. I'd bring him inside and make him lie down on the couch. Easier to keep and eye on him there. I'd monitor his pulse and such too.

One day, I was putting laundry away. I found drugs in his sock drawer. Lucky for him, he was at work when I found them because I was so angry. I had calmed down by the time he did come home. But we did have a very serious conversation. I explained to him that I couldn't be around those drugs because of my job and my paramedic license. The drugs could make me quickly lose both. I also reminded him of his DUI and that his probation officer could show up at any time, search the place, and he'd go to jail. I said that I'd also go to jail because I live there and that I'm not going to jail for something I didn't do. He said he understood and sincerely apologized. He said that it was just a once in a while habit, but that he would stop. Earlier I had thrown the baggie of drugs in the trash and told him so. Then I told him one of the most difficult things I have ever had to say in my life. I said that if I ever found drugs in the house again, I would have to leave because I can't be around it. He looked at me and nodded that he understood. That almost emotionally killed me to have to say that.

I thought things were good then. By now it was February 2015. I began working on taxes and was excited that I could file as married instead of single. I mentioned that to him one day. He looked at me all serious and said, "I have a confession". He then proceeded to tell me that he hadn't filed taxes in several years and owed a fairly decent amount of money to Uncle Sam. I looked at him dumbfounded.

Could there be anything else wrong with this dude? First the drinking, then the drugs, and now this? I had a gut feeling on the honeymoon that I had made the wrong decision because he was drinking so heavily. I had to tell him to slow down or we wouldn't have gas money to get home. I had felt like I had to be the adult and babysitter on the honeymoon. What a way to start out right.

I struggled with what to do. First off, I filed my own taxes as single and left him out of it. But then what about the rest? What do you do when your spouse admits that he is basically doing illegal activity? I talked to him several times. He knew he was in the wrong. I helped him get into counseling, but he refused to do what his counselor told him to do. He would come home and tell me what his counselor said. It was exactly what I wanted to tell him but couldn't because he wasn't hearing me. I decided to wait a bit longer. I knew there would be an out eventually.

Sure enough, several months later, I found the same baggie of drugs again. He had dug them out of the trash. Oh how I cried. I cried like never before because I knew what I had to do next. I wasn't going to be able to stay here anymore. I took the baggie outside and destroyed it. Oh how I was pissed off!

I was still very worked up and pissed when he arrived home from work. I never yelled at him. I just calmly told him about finding the drugs AGAIN and asked him why. He had no legitimate answer. I reminded him that I couldn't stay there when there are drugs in the house. He tried to tell me that the bag was the only stash and such. How do you believe a drug addict?

I left with my bags packed. I told him I would get the rest of my things later when I could. I went to a friend's house. I cried so much. It hurt so much having to do this. I had to leave my best friend and turn my back on him. I had done everything I knew to do to try to help him, but he had wanted none of it. What I hoped would happen was that he would realize what was happening and decide to get help. I was hoping that he would see how serious this was. Would he? Or was this just a big joke to him? Would we get back together? Or would our relationship end in divorce?

Chapter 16

My Divorce

Where do you turn?

Where do you turn when your world is falling apart?

Where do you turn when everything around you is crumbling?

Where do you turn when your ship is sinking?

Where do you turn when you feel as if you're falling apart?

Where do you turn when the darkness is creeping in?

Where do you turn when your light is dimming?

Where do you turn when the struggles seem to rule your life?

Where do you turn when the waves are trying to drown you?

Where do you turn when people choose to walk out of your life?

WHere do you turn when your worries overtake your thoughts?

I turn to the arms that carry me.

I turn to the captain of my ship.

I turn to those who have chosen to stick by me.

I turn towards the light away from the darkness.

I turn to all the positives that have come from this.

I turn to my inner strength.

I turn to to find someone who needs a listening ear and encouragement.

I turn to the shore and keep swimming towards it.

I turn my thoughts towards the positive.

I turn to the new day ahead and what it may bring.

For I can get through this.

I will never give up.

I will never give in.

For it's 5 minutes at a time.

-BonniferWW

How would you react if your spouse left you because of illegal things you were doing? Would you realize what you were doing was wrong? Would you decide to get help? Would you throw temper tantrums like a child? Would you be angry and destroy items left in your house that belonged to her?

Well, he acted like a child. He told me I was being immature and needed to come back home so that we could work things out. He told me that he wasn't going to get help. He told me that getting my own apartment was a major drastic move.

I told him that if he was willing to go into inpatient drug and alcohol rehabilitation, then I'd come home. I said that I was willing to go work enough overtime to pay the bills while he was in rehab and to not worry about a thing. It would all be taken care of. He continued to refuse. I decided to give him some time to see if he would change his mind before I filed for divorce.

I began looking for an apartment. I asked around, but no one knew of one at that exact moment. A few hours later, one of my firemen buddies, Kenny, texted me back and said that one he knew of suddenly became available. He put me in touch with the owners…. Kyle and Amanda. The apartment was a mother-in-law suite attached to the back of their house.

Now Kenny filled me in on why it had suddenly become available. He said that the resident had suddenly hung himself inside the apartment. Kyle had gone back to check on him and had found him hanging. I was shocked because that was the last thing I had been expecting. How do you react to something like that right? Would you still live in an apartment or house knowing someone had committed suicide in there? Or would you find somewhere else?

Well, I figured I'd at least go look and see how I felt about the matter. I went and met Amanda and Kyle. Turned out that I already knew Kyle from when I worked at the Tulsa ambulance service. He was a Tulsa firefighter. I looked at the apartment and loved it actually. Amanda told me the story too about the hanging. I did ask where he had hung himself and she told me it had been in the staircase.

I decided to sign the lease for the apartment. It would be a couple weeks before it was ready since the family still had to come and get the guys things out. I was totally fine with that. My friend Lisa, with whom I'd been staying, was fine with it also.

I told Charley, just to update him on things. He again threw a temper tantrum. I tried so hard just to ignore his behavior. I reminded him I wasn't filing for divorce yet but would soon unless he changed his mind about things.

All of this was seriously hurting me emotionally. Every single day. It affected me in everything I did. It was difficult to get out of bed every day, to go to work, even to get done the things I needed to regularly. It affected my patient care and attitude at work. I had trouble concentrating at times. I was short-tempered too. I was less patient. The guys I worked with were very understanding and were great listeners. They were there to help me through it.

I was so tired of having to work 90 plus hours a week just to pay the bills. Charley would only work 40 hours a week if that. Most weeks there were days he'd come home early "because he was bored". He wouldn't get paid for those hours. So I was left to make up those hours. He always talked about getting a part-time job, but never did.

I had waited approximately eight weeks and Charley was still the same. His attitude was still the same. He still refused to get help. I decided it was time to file for divorce. This was also one of the most difficult things I had ever done. I told him what the plan was and of course this made him angry again, but he did nothing and gave no reason to stop.

I called a few lawyers in Tulsa, but never heard back from them. So I called a lawyer up in Bartlesville where we had lived together. Finally a real person answered the phone. I made an appointment and went in. I explained the situation and filed the paperwork. I had to come up with $1,000. He said he would let me make payments so my overtime pay was going toward my divorce for a bit. I wanted to have this done before Christmas as a present to myself.

I worked hard in overtime. I made several payments and got it done. I celebrated as soon as my last payment was made. But now I had to go to court. I had never been to court before. I was scared as could be. What happens in court? Do you really have to stand at a stand before a judge? Is it a long process? Can I take someone with me into the courtroom? Is it all formal?

Well, the day came. I was a huge emotional mess. I took my friend Malik with me. Now I had been to the courthouse before for our marriage license. I knew what it looked like. I had driven by it dozens of times. I knew where it was. But that day, it didn't look like the courthouse. It looked like a different building because I was that worked up and nervous. Malik had to convince me it was the courthouse. I still made him go ask someone if it was the courthouse.

We went inside and found my lawyer. He told me the process and what would happen. Thank goodness it wasn't going to be a courtroom, but would just be the judge's office. Malik would have to stay outside though. "Okay, I can do this", I thought to myself. I seriously just wanted to go hide and cry my eyes out though. The judge was very nice and understanding of the situation. The whole thing was short, and to the point.

Afterwards, Malik and I went back to the car, and I cried on his shoulder in total relief that it was over and maybe a little sadness that my marriage had ended. There was also brokenness because I had officially lost my best friend basically forever, and a celebration because I was out of that mess. I didn't have to worry about the police showing up and going to jail for something I didn't do. I didn't have to worry about him driving drunk and getting another DUI. I didn't have to worry about getting that phone call again from the jail saying that he was in jail and he needed bail money.

I had met my goal of giving myself a huge Christmas present. Though I still had the major emotions to deal with, and the other issues too, I was a free woman. I knew it was time to take care of me for a good while. It was time to focus on my goals and dreams for once.

Maybe I could take myself out on dates. Maybe I could take myself on road trips across the country looking for awesome half and full marathons. Maybe I could actually save some money. Maybe I wouldn't have to work so many hours.

Oh yeah, what did my parents think of all of this? This is comical to me so I thought I'd add it. First off, they were not supportive. The whole time, they told me I should be trying things I had already tried…. talking to him, counseling, etc. Then when I left him, they were okay with that, but insisted again on counseling. I told them again that he was refusing counseling and rehab. But when I filed for the divorce, HOLY CRAP!, you would have thought that the wrath of God was going to come down and strike me through lightning or something, according to Mom and Dad. They were angry. I asked them, "So basically, I'm supposed to stay in an abusive marriage no matter what?" That's what it was really. They told me, "Yes, absolutely because God and the bible are against divorce." I call total bullshit! You have to protect yourself first and if you have kids, your kids, too. Their opinion upset me a little, but mostly I had to laugh. I just felt sorry for them.

There will be a tomorrow!

When it hurts,

When everything hurts,

Where do you turn?

Where do you go?

When it pains,

When it pains you to tears,

Where do you turn?

Where do you go?

When you're stuck,

When you're stuck on what to do,

Where do you turn?

Where do you go?

When you can't,

When you can't take another step,

Where do you turn?

Where do you go?

When your mind,

When your mind seems to never slow,

Where do you turn?

Where do you go?

As I lay here now in my own thoughts,

It is not without struggles,

It is not without tears,

It is not without fear,

It is not without headache.

What is next?

What is next I must face?

What is next?

What is next I must beat?

What is next?

What is next I must overcome?

I'm scared.

I'm nervous.

I'm frightened.

I'm crying.

I'm screaming.

BUT

5...10...20...YEARS FROM NOW

I can look back and say

I was there!

I accepted the challenge!

I asked for help when needed!

I grew!

I fought!

I was carried by so many!

I kept fighting

I learned to take life 5 minutes at a time!

Keep fighting!

Struggle! Fight!

Cry! Overcome!

Scream! Face it!

Just take it 5 minutes at a time

Don't ever give up!

Don't ever give in!

-BonniferWW

Chapter 17

Beginning my Life at Mercy

If

I wouldn't have made it this far

If you had treated me as some have,

If you had pushed me away,

If you had ignored my need.

I wouldn't have been this strong

If you hadn't carried me,

If you hadn't helped me,

If you hadn't loved me.

I wouldn't have fought so hard

If you hadn't fought with me,

If you hadn't bandaged my wounds,

If you hadn't been my strength.

I wouldn't have felt this loved

If you hadn't made me giggle when the tears were imminent,

If you hadn't hugged me tight,

If you hadn't walked that race with me.

I wouldn't have felt this whole

If you hadn't helped to glue the pieces back together,

If you hadn't allowed me to cry on your shoulder,

If you hadn't seen my potential even in the darkness.

I wouldn't have wanted to live

If you hadn't been my lifeline,

If you hadn't helped me find a purpose,

If you hadn't seen past what I couldn't.

I wouldn't be here in the now

If you hadn't supported me,

If you hadn't showed up when i wanted to be alone,

If you hadn't hung on to my hand in the storm.

I wouldn't be who I am at this moment

If you hadn't seen past my frustration and anger,

If you had given up on me,

If you had left me alone for forever.

Because of you

I know I will make it another five minutes,

I know that, while i will fall, you'll help me up,

I know that I will never ever be alone.

-BonniferWW

I had lined up an interview at Mercy Regional EMS at the end of my two year contract at the Tulsa ambulance service. I needed something with a legit and consistent pay scale. I didn't need to receive a pay raise and then have it taken away later. Or any of the rest of the things the Tulsa ambulance service was beginning to do. Now, yes, there are crazy politics anywhere you go, especially there. I knew there would be at Mercy, too. I needed a break from the world of the Tulsa ambulance service.

I went to my interview and it was one of the easiest interviews I've ever had really. In the interview, I was asked if I wanted rotating 24 hr shifts or if I wanted a 48-hour shift with 5 days off. Pfffftttt That was easy. I said I wanted the 48hr shift. It was out in Vinita OK.... aka small-town America, but it covered all of Craig county. I was so excited. I was still married at this point, so I called Charley afterwards. I was stoked!

I did a couple third rides just to learn the paperwork. Now on my first day, I rode with a crew who will remain nameless. It was on a 12-hour day shift truck and it was basically transfers all day. I was fine with that. The paramedic gave me the computer and said "Okay, here ya go. Do the paperwork." No explanation of the charting system or anything. I thought to myself, "Okay, I got this".

I punched and typed away on that computer working on the patient's run tickets for the day. It was almost the end of our shift before we had time for my paramedic to look over my run tickets and how I was doing on them. When she did look them over, let's just say that she belittled me greatly for not finding all the hidden things that are supposed to be filled in.....you know, the things that you don't know are even there unless you've used this particular charting program before. If you've done this type of charting before, you know exactly what I'm talking about. Unless you're a para-God, you've been there yourself.

I almost walked off the job that night. Almost! I thought to myself that if this is the attitude and treatment that they allow their paramedics to have of others, then I want no part of it. I was hot! I almost called up the big boss and told him so too. When we got back to the station, I walked around to calm down a bit which helped. I reminded myself that this was the only ride I would ever have to do with this particular paramedic, though I could begin to pray for her future third riders that she would have mercy on their poor beings. I reminded myself that I had the best shift ever coming to me just around the corner and in small town america. I love small towns. I also reminded myself that if I quit this one, I'd have to go find another one. Then I told myself to knock it off and chill the fuck out. It was okay. Nice pep talk huh, and that's a tame one.

Then I was sent out to Vinita for a couple third rides just to start learning the area before being on my own. VInita ran with 2 ambulances. One was in Big Cabin and was responsible for non-emergency transfers, that side of the county 911 calls, and then the back-up truck for 911 calls for Vinita. The Vinita truck did 911 calls and then emergency transfers from the hospital. Sounded perfect to me. I would be on the Big Cabin truck.

I met my EMT Cody. He seemed pretty cool. He looked like Thor, too. I settled in and things were going well. Cody and I worked well together. We were in sync and knew what the other was going to do without a word. Cody later said, "I remember the first time I met you in Big Cabin. I was in awe of how many years of experience you had as a medic. I was nervous to be so green to the profession, I didn't want to embarrass you, or make your job tougher. Those were the thoughts that ran through my head on one of the first calls we went to that wasn't even in our area."

We ran some good calls together. We had a patient who was mad at their mate. Patient had kicked a rock because of the situation. Being drunk didn't help either. Or the patient that was trying to push a couch up a ladder to the second floor by using their leg. Said leg was broken. Or sitting down at a local restaurant for a meal only to find a local patron also eating at the same restaurant who began experiencing a stroke while there. We met the life-flight crew at the airport.

There were high school football games where we did stand-by and would just talk BS with each other to watching movies at the station such as "Ernest Scared Stupid" to going to the gym for a workout. But then Cody also said this to me, "I remember the mass car wreck on the highway. The semi-trailer that was blown over by the tornado. I remember going to the jail, to the young women's rehabilitation center, and going to Bluejacket and Welch. I remember the real heart attacks, the suicides, and the overdoses. I remember more about how awesome you are, when you dressed up and acted like a fool to make someone laugh. I remember how encouraging you are. How bad ass you are. I remember the good times more so than any bad ones."

Cody was the best partner I ever had working at Mercy. He helped me a lot when I was going through my divorce. He was one of the guys that came and helped me move my stuff too. He and I are still very good friends today.

After a while, Craig county decided that they were building a new ambulance barn and it would house both ambulances. There would no longer be a truck in Big Cabin. Every time an employee would ask about a finish or move in date, we were told "2 weeks". Always! But it would be months. We would ask our immediate supervisor. "2 weeks." Someone else on a different shift would ask a different supervisor. "2 weeks." Well, it was the week right before Thanksgiving that year. We were able to cook Thanksgiving dinner in the new station that year…...barely.

You never know who you may have as a patient either. It may be a coworker, a friend, someone you know well from the community, or it could be someone you used to work with in a different state. It's a Thursday morning and Cody and I are just coming on shift. While we're checking our truck, my phone starts ringing with text messages from an old EMT partner, Jim. Jim was now a OTR trucker. I didn't pay much mind to it because it was usually him asking if I was making cookies just in case he came through Oklahoma even though he could be up in Rhode Island or Maine or wherever. Before I had a chance to look, the tones dropped, and we were on the way to our first call for chest pain out at the truck stop. Probably some poor trucker having health issues. Then I glanced at my phone. Yep, it's a trucker alright. It's my old EMT buddy Jim. I told Cody.

We arrived on scene and found the OHP trooper car with the semi. Now normally, I do not speak to my patients this way, just the patients I love and care about like family. Jim stepped out of the police officer's vehicle, looked officially like crud, and had that "I'm scared" and "I'm so glad you're a familiar face" looks on his face. I said, "Get your ass in the truck!!!" The police officer looked at me a bit shocked because he even knew me better than that. I told me that we used to work together back in Indiana. He just started chuckling.

We began our assessment and treatment. Vitals, EKG, monitor, IV, baby aspirin, nitro, oxygen, the works. Jim then proceeded to tell me that he had driven an hour out of his way to get to me just so he could see a familiar face because that's how scared and nervous he was about the chest pain and other symptoms he was having. I told him that as a friend I completely understood, but as a paramedic I was going to give him a chewing out session he'd never forget......while we were on the way to the hospital of course. No delaying of treatment for an ass chewing. Actually, I told him I was pulling the big sister card, the former ems partner card, and forgot what else, but he knew better than to drive an hour while possibly having a heart attack. I would have clobbered him if it had been more serious than it was. Turned out that his blood pressure was just crazy out of control, but everything else was great. The emergency room kept him for a while for observation. Oh and he did get a batch of Oatmeal Raisin Cookies before he hit the road again. Road trips, whether working road trips or fun, are always better with homemade cookies on board.

Chapter 18

Vinita Life

Why? What? Where? How?

Why can't my life be easy?

Why can't I catch a break?

Why must I carry this burden?

How much more do I have to get through?

What am I supposed to do?

What am I supposed to accomplish?

What am I supposed to learn?

How much more do I have to get through?

Where do I turn when I can't take anymore?

Where do I go when I walk into darkness?

Where do I turn to find something good?

How much more do I have to get through?

Why have I been chosen to go down this path?

Why do I have to suffer for someone else's choices?

Why must I be the one to be left alone in the dirt?

How much more do I have to get through?

What am I going to do to live?

What kind of life will I be able to have?

What if I must always depend upon others for my needs?

How much more do I have to take?

Where do I go from here?

Where do I find the strength to go on when I'm empty?

Where must I go to find relief?

How much more do I have to take?

I'm having a rough moment.

I'm struggling.

I'm fighting to continue.

I'm discouraged.

What is the point of these nightmares?

What is the meaning of all this?

What will be the outcome?

What can I do to change my circumstances?

Maybe the next moment will be better.

Maybe tomorrow will be brighter., I am not a failure.

Maybe I'll be stronger in a while.

Maybe my next step will be a bit lighter.

Hopefully it will be better in the next five minutes.

Hopefully the sun will shine brighter.

Hopefully the weight will lighten.

Hopefully something huge and great will develop from this.

I know I'm being carried through this.

I know that while I will fail, I am not a failure.

I know that things will get better one step at a time.

I know that today is not my end.

-BonniferWW

Working in Vinita was great. Working in a small town and county was also great because I loved getting to know many of the people by running calls, through going to Walmart, and frequent community events. There was an elderly couple who we began to run on frequently due to diabetes. On a particular shift, I had made cookies. That Friday, both crews decided to go visit them outside of a 911 call and take them some cookies. We thought that if we took them some cookies, maybe we wouldn't have to run on them that night. We had run on them the last two Friday nights in a row. Yes, we all knew that diabetics shouldn't have that much sugar, but we did it anyway. Irresponsible? Maybe. Caring about our patient? Yes.

We showed up and of course they were surprised but were excited for the company. They didn't get many visitors. We stayed for maybe 20 minutes and visited. Little did we know that was just the beginning of a lifelong relationship. We continued to run on them every few shifts.

For the following, I do have permission to put in patient details. I have permission from the wife, Mrs. Lilly C. She gets confused and doesn't remember things, but she was very lucid when I asked her.

Bill continued to struggle with his blood sugar. Then he found out he had lung cancer and six months to live. He ended up living for two years longer. As he began to weaken, my EMT and I (sometimes the other crew too) would go check on both of them every shift. See if they need anything or help doing something.

They decided to move down to Texas so that Lilly would be close to their son after Bill passed. I was super sorry to see them go. I was just starting to get a little close to Miss Lilly. That's what I always called her and eventually, everyone else did too. It was always Bill and Miss Lilly. After being down there only a couple months, they moved back. But we had no clue about this.

One night, we received a call for an unconscious diabetic at a different address then where they had initially lived. We didn't think anything of it. Then we showed up and it was Bill that needed help. I was happy to see them, but first Bill needed to be tended to.

We had Bill awake and eating a peanut butter sandwich in no time. Then we chatted with both of them. Turns out, they hated it in Austin and decided to move back. Bill was feeling worse and weaker. One could tell by looking at him. Miss Lilly looked a little older from the stress of it all. So once again, I began my weekly visits to check on them.

I took a week off just before Christmas. The next week back, we'd been too busy with calls that we didn't get a chance to go by and check on them. So I stopped by on the way home after shift. I knocked on the door. Miss Lilly answered. I could tell by the look on her face that something had drastically changed. I went inside. She told me that Bill had passed about a week before. My eyes watered a bit and told her that I hadn't heard yet. No one had heard at the station that I knew of. I gave her a big hug and made very sure that she didn't need anything. She assured me she didn't.

I left that day feeling heavy hearted. I texted Julie and told her. I texted a couple crews that worked before I would be back for my next shift asking them to please check on her if at all possible. She needed to be checked on and be around people. She had no family in Vinita. From this point on, I checked on her every single shift. If I didn't make it over on shift, I stopped by before I drove home. We became very close over the next couple years. She became like a grandmother but would get mad if I called her "Grandma". She told me I could call her "Mom".

Then there was the required "Happy Hour" at the hospital. We were required by management to go to the hospital for an hour and hang out. Help them if they are busy or just talk and get to know them. Let them get to know us. It was grand. Sure, sometimes we were too busy to make it there for an hour. Sometimes, we'd be there and get a call. Cody and I were great at doing this and even enjoyed it. Some of my partners refused to do it. Management also grew slack at requiring it.

There were many community events in Vinita that I made sure my EMT and I were involved in. From the rodeo to the parades to the high school football games to bull testicle festival to the kids and cops day to the annual 5ks to so much more. It was incredible how many things the town of Vinita was able to put on. There was always something to do, or something to plan to do, or something to look forward to.

Chapter 19

Vinita EMS Partners

Just dead!

What if you died

And lived not through the night?

What if you took that last breath,

With not another one to ever take?

What if you were as follows.....

Just Dead!

Would your beautiful soul be remembered?

Would your life story long be forever shared?

Would your memory never be forgotten?

Keep living!

Keep rocking it!

Keep showing who's boss!

-BonniferWW

In EMS, you have several partners based upon how the
service runs. Some departments run so that you have a
different partner every shift. Some run where you change
partners every few months or so. While at others, you could
have the same partners for years. At Mercy, you could have
the same partner for years. Only reasons why you wouldn't is
if someone quit, was fired, or changed shifts.

Of course there was Cody, but after Cody, there was Danielle.
Danielle was a very green EMT aka new EMT. She was great
though. She was quick to learn, loved our patients, great

driver, and good to be around the station with. She also went with me willingly to Miss Lily's. She was willing to get involved in community events too. Her side job was as a wedding photographer and she was great at it too. She ran her own business. I always told her that if I ever got married again, that I was going to book her as my photographer. That still stands by the way.

My next partner was Jon. He was a volunteer firefighter also, but not in Vinita.

He had two small boys and a wife. He was very experienced and loved the ambulance, but he loved fighting fires more. We were partners for several months, but he was always looking for a better job to support his family. He ended up leaving after he found that job that paid more than double what he was making as an EMT. If I remember right, it was also more than double of what I was making at the time.

Next, I had probably one of the worst partners in my career. He was definitely in the top 5. His name is Deppy. He was very experienced and had also worked at the Tulsa ambulance service. So he should have known better in many instances. We ran a call together on a semi-conscious patient. I had to tell him literally everything to hand me or do or to get ready. "Deppy, take a blood pressure." "Deppy, pass the monitor over please." He only placed it on the bed out of my reach. "Deppy, can you please get IV stuff ready for me out of the trauma bag?" He did but didn't hand me anything to tape it down with. He had disappeared out to the truck for I don't know what. So I'm stuck holding the IV in the patient's arm while I try to stretch across to reach the trauma bag to get some tape. Finally, a family member comes in and helps me.

Eventually Deppy comes back. By this time, I'm ready to load up the patient onto the cot. He had an attitude at this point for an unknown reason. Of course he had an attitude most of the call too. Maybe he forgot his meds or something. I don't know. Anyway, we got the patient loaded and I told him to just go ahead and drive us to the hospital. I would do the rest of the procedures on the way. The patient didn't need the attitude and I sure didn't want it. Nor did I have the patience for it. There were many calls we ran like this where he had an attitude issue for an unknown reason.

Then one shift, I came to work extremely sick with pneumonia. Thing is when a paramedic calls off work, the community suffers. Plus we were allowed to use medications and fluids as needed for ourselves if we were on shift, but unofficially. I could do breathing nebulizer treatments and steroid shots at work if I was at work. So for 48 hours, I just struggled to breathe and survive my shift. I ran a call, did the paperwork, and went back to bed. That was my life for those 48 hours.

After that shift, I got a call from management asking me if I knew anything about the major dent in the shelves in the back of the ambulance. I told them no. I said I had been really sick and had been just trying to breathe the whole shift. I told them because of that, I was in the back of the truck much less than normal. Deppy had done all of the restocking and such.

That wasn't the only phone call. I received a few more phone calls. I was even called into the office. Each time, it was basically the same conversation. In the office, I was told they wanted me to feel safe telling them what really happened. They told me that the damage had been traced to my shift. I told them again what happened. I also told them that I didn't like Deppy and couldn't stand him. I said that if I had seen him do anything that I would gladly have told them, but since I hadn't seen anything actually happen, I couldn't tell them. Management finally seemed content with that answer.

My next shift with Deppy, he seemed extremely irritated with me. I told him exactly what had happened. I also told him what I had said. He said he didn't believe me, but I didn't care. I knew I had done the right thing. I also knew he was guilty. He told me that he was probably on the verge of getting fired and it was all my fault. I said to him that he shouldn't have thrown the oxygen bottle into the cabinet. Silence. You could have heard a pin drop.

The truth will always be found out! The truth will set you free!

Chapter 20

Mick

I have a purpose

There are no words to describe the pain...

You claimed you were my friend.

There are no words to describe the agony...

You claimed you cared about me.

There are no words to describe the suffering...

You claimed I was your rock.

There are no words to describe the hardship...

You claimed you were my big brother.

There are no words to describe the darkness...

You claimed you were my work husband.

There are no words to describe the sorrow...

You claimed you were my family.

There are no words in the English language to describe what you have done.

Even cuss/swear words are too good for the likes of you.

You planned for months to also take my life when you took yours.

You worked for months building up an image that never existed.

Yet, through it all, you have failed miserably.

While you failed at being my friend, I've discovered who my best friends truly are.

While you failed at being your true self, I've begun to discover who I truly am.

While you failed at honesty, I've gotten completely honest with myself and others.

While you failed at being my family, your actions have brought my true family even closer.

While you failed horribly at the attempt to take my life, I am discovering what life is truly about.

For my time here is not completed.

For my job here is not done.

For I have something left to do.

Yes, being mad at you doesn't even begin to cover the emotions that roll through me.

But, I have a purpose and that can never be taken from me.

-BonniferWW

Where do you begin the story of the man who attempted to murder you? How do you remember the good times before the incident? How can the "good times" not be tarnished and affected? When I try to think of the memories beforehand, I still get pissed off. Maybe it's because now I know he was living a double life. Maybe it's because I know it was all a lie. Maybe it's because I wonder if there was any truth in it at all. Was he honest at all? Anything?

He told me that he had been in the military, but that his mom didn't even know. No one in his family knew. He told me that he had helped with many natural disasters pulling bodies out of the water and defending particular areas. He said that he was in EMS to pay for his sins. Was it truth or lies?

He said that he had started chemotherapy. He said that he was close to his mom. He said I would be well taken care of after he was gone. Was it all lies or was there any truth?

We did work well together on the truck. People even asked if we were a couple to which I always replied with a big NO. I explained that we had just been coworker partners for a long time and were close. We didn't have to talk but knew exactly what the other would do.

One time we had a young driver who had low blood sugar. This driver had been pulled over for erratic driving. The officer realized what had happened and called EMS. We arrived and assessed the situation. We got the patient's blood sugar up and then the patient refused to be transported to the hospital. We told the patient they needed to eat something asap to which they stated they had no money and only had enough to get to Mom's house which was a good 100 miles away. I called the mother and explained the situation and told her that the patient was okay and would be back on the way shortly. Then we gave the patient $20 to get food and some gas. We sent them on their way.

Now when we had any possible combative patients, sometimes they would respond better to Mick and sometimes better to me. If they responded better to Mick, then I would drive. We would go straight to the little hospital in Vinita. We rarely would do anything to these patients. Max would be a blood pressure if tolerated. One time we were called to one of the mentally handicapped homes for a patient who claimed he had been poisoned at lunch. Staff stated that the patient had done this before and that he had eaten the same thing everyone else had. Everyone else was fine.

Patient was standing outside and had his hands balled up into fists swinging his arms. I talked to staff while Mick walked him to the truck. The two of them talked and Mick was able to calm him down.

This was one instance when I drove. I picked up the radio to tell dispatch that we were transporting. I said it in my normal voice and not panicked at all or anything. We drove calmly and easily to the hospital. We began to notice that we suddenly had a police escort. Upon arrival at the hospital, there were also several police officers waiting for us. We hadn't had one lick of trouble from the patient, so we didn't know what the trouble was. The officers walked with us inside. Of course the patient was freaking out a little. We told the patient they were just there to hang out and check on the emergency room staff to which seemed to make it okay.

Turned out that, due to the nature of the call, when dispatch heard me driving, they assumed that Mick was in the back getting his ass kicked so they went ahead and called for police assistance. I'd much rather than not have them or not be able to get a hold of dispatch or the dispatcher being a goober demanding to know why we need them before dispatching them. Yes, all of those have happened. We were getting our butts kicked a couple different times and were telling dispatch we needed help ASAP. Dispatch, instead of immediately putting in the request for help, wanted to know exactly what was happening, why we needed help, and who we thought we needed. Sometimes, it was easier just to fight the patient and drive the three minutes to the hospital than to argue with dispatch.

I remember when Mick first found out he had prostate cancer. It was shortly before his 50th birthday. The plan was that he would have surgery to remove his prostate. He was far from happy about it, but his doctor's thought this would completely get rid of the cancer.

Speaking of his birthday, no one in his life had been able to pull off a surprise birthday party for him. EVER! I was determined to. I engaged the help of one of his former partners. Her and her husband took care of providing the meat and inviting some of his family. I took care of the cake and decorations. Others provided the sides.

When it got close, I told Mick that I was going to take him out for his birthday. At first he agreed to it. Then the shift right before, I reminded him. He told me he couldn't because he had to work, that he wanted me to save my money, and that I didn't need to be spending my money on him. I argued back telling him that this was really important to me and that he was a special guy and that he shouldn't be working so much on his birthday. I told him whatever kind of nonsense I could think of to talk him into it. He finally agreed. Then the day before, I called him just to make sure. He tried again to get out of it. This time, I didn't ask. I told. I told him I was picking him up at his house at 6pm sharp the next day. I told him he had better be there and had better be ready. I reminded him that this was seriously important to me. He said "Okay".

The next day, I was at his house 6:00 pm sharp. He was there and ready to go. He got in my car and of course, immediately wanted to know where we were going for dinner. I told him it was a surprise and that we had reservations. He kept telling me that I didn't need to do this and blah blah blah. I basically told him to shut up. Hehehe

I mentioned that we had to stop by the Vinita EMS station because I had forgotten my car charger from last shift. He didn't know I had left it there on purpose as an excuse to go there. We had to wait for a train, and while waiting for that train, we saw the supervisor vehicle. In my head I said, "OH CRAP!". Mick saw the vehicle too and then commented wondering what the boss was doing in town so late. It wasn't normal.

After the train, we continued to the station. As we rounded the corner, we both saw the fire truck parked in the side drive.....also far from normal. By now the supervisor vehicle was also parked. Mick looked at me and said, "What have you done?" I just started laughing and cheering because I had actually pulled it off. Then I looked at him and said, "Happy Birthday". I told him that I wanted him to know how many people were behind him and supporting him through this cancer fight.

We went inside then. I watched his face as we entered. He was fighting back tears as he went around and gave people hugs. He was speechless and didn't have much to say. I was flying high because we had managed to pull it off. It was so freaking awesome. Incredible!!!

So on the other hand, yes we were close. Yes, he was like a brother to me. Yes, I was like a little sister to him. He even called me "sis". He cried on my shoulder as needed at work. Not just a little cry either. It was sobbing.

Sometime before the shooting, he had taken one of my checks from my checkbook that was in my car. He wrote it to the family business for $850. I had no knowledge of this. When I got out of the hospital and was able to get my new phone set up again....and remembered all my passwords.....I looked at my bank account and saw that this check had bounced twice while I was in the hospital. I immediately panicked and called Discover. I thought we had gotten it all taken care of.

Even now, almost three years later, I still cannot understand how you go from close friend to attempted murderer in 3.2 seconds. How does that happen? How can you pretend to care for someone that deeply? Was the response at the birthday party just an act?

Mick then got cancer a second time. He didn't talk much about it this time. He just said that the docs said it was behind his thyroid this time. His left arm would randomly go numb. He began vomiting several times a day but would blame it on his medications. He stopped eating as much. He lost a lot of weight. I knew without him saying anything. I knew the cancer was much more widespread than just behind his thyroid. I also knew he didn't have much time left.

I knew his way of going out of this world would be suicide. I knew it would be. He told me once long before the incident that if he's deathly sick, in his mind, he's a sick animal. When an animal is that sick, you take it out and shoot it. He said that in his mind, he's an animal. I never thought he'd try to hurt anyone in the process.

Several months later, I decided to volunteer at St. Francis Hospital in Vinita in the emergency room. One or two nights a week with four-hour shifts. It completely wore me out, but it forced me out of the house, and it gave me time with my people. When I applied, I failed my background check because I had a warrant out for my arrest due to the bounced check. I completely freaked out. Imagine that right. So I went to see a lawyer friend I knew who was a local volunteer fireman, also. He helped me get it fixed after I found several items with my signature on it. We proved that my real signature did not match the signature on the check. We got the warrant removed. Whew!!!!

Chapter 21

The Rest of the Story

TBI

I cannot skip

Rocks, my feet, or my class

I cannot toodaloo

My fingers, my eyes, or my pinky

I cannot drive

A car, a bus, a train

But I can drive my sister insane.

I cannot work

In EMS, in the ER, or on a boat

I cannot save your life

So you hold my beer instead

And watch this.....oh wait!

I cannot intubate.

I cannot cardiovert.

I cannot defibrillate.

I cannot run

In a park, in a gym, or in a marathon.

I cannot jump small or tall or in between.

For the fall from the run or the jump would be small or tall or in between.

I cannot remember what it is that I just said.

I cannot work.....I cannot run.....I cannot toodaloo.

Well, FUDGE!

But I do love me some homemade fudge.

My appetite stinks.

My hearing sucks.

And now I'm OCD.

What the WHAT is this we've got?

They tell me it's a TBI.

I say it's a …..Well, I can't say that here.

My head hurts.

They say it might always will.

What will we do then Vern?

I suppose you'll keep saying what you've always said these last two years.

What is that Vern?

Damn it Vern!

I cannot eat

Raw fish, my arm, or a can of spam.

I cannot eat

What is in the fridge, the cabinet, or the lint catcher.

For I have no appetite

For the good, the odd, or the insane food.

I cannot remember what it is that I just said.

For now my brain is all screwy and bullet fragment filled.

What will we do Vern?

I cannot jump small, tall, or in between

And I will most likely always have a long list of issues.

To the conclusion I've come

That while I may never

Run, drive, work, skip, toodaloo, jump,

Or even have more than a half working brain again,

There will ALWAYS be beer.

There will ALWAYS be fudge.

And there will FLIPPING ALWAYS be marathons.

-BonniferWW

Now, almost three years later, the parents have not come to visit. They have only talked about it. Again, what kind of parents do that to their child? We have always had a rocky and difficult relationship, but that shouldn't matter when your child is fighting for her life and should be dead. Would you show up to your child's hospital bedside? How much would have to happen to your child before you'd decide to show up? A minor car wreck? A broken leg? Something to land in ICU? I'm not a parent so I can't really say what a parent should do or how much it should take. But I do know that a parent should be at the bedside when a child is fighting the Grim Reaper. That is for sure!

What happened next you ask? I'm sure you're dying to know after having had to read so many chapters to find out. Well, here goes. On one hand, I had hoped the parents would show up, but on the other I was glad they hadn't. I did tell people with me and staff that I didn't want to be left alone if they showed up. I was concerned there would be too much drama.

I was later told the following story by Amanda. She told it much better than I can. She said that the nurses were trying to get lots of information from me, from demographics to what happened. I went in circles telling them the same thing over and over. Amanda said she was in the corner dying laughing. Meanwhile, I'm telling the nurses that I don't want my parents in the room because I'm not wearing pants. Over and over again. "I don't want my parents in here because I'm not wearing pants." "I don't want my parents in here because I'm not wearing pants." Amanda explained to the nurses that my relationship with my parents was not good. Eventually she had to help the nurses get information from me by asking me direct questions herself and asking them very simplified. Some questions had to wait until my sister arrived.

I was so dizzy that it took two people to help me stand up and walk to the bathroom. There was a catheter in place for a bit and was removed by the time my sister arrived. At least it seemed that way. She helped me to the restroom a lot, even cleaned me because both my hands were majorly wrapped up due to the severe damage on both. Now that's true love right there. Yep.

I began physical therapy every day. My physical therapist brought me a walker. The walker had arm rests on it, and it turned out to be the best thing ever. With that walker, I was able to be a little bit independent. I walked those hallways like a pro.....well a pro who'd been shot in the head anyhow. I always had someone with me though...whether it was my therapist or it was a visitor. Every time a visitor showed up, which was often, I'd ask them if they wanted to walk with me. Sometimes it was a yes and other times, it was not so much.

I was in the hospital for eight days. Each day I fought off severe pain, nightmares, and depression. Each day I grew a little stronger. Each day was a little better than the day before. One day, while still in the hospital, one of my visitors noticed I had left-sided facial droop. She notified the nurse, and I was immediately taken for a CAT scan. I had had a stroke along with my other injuries of a skull fracture, finger fractures, head bleed, and seizures. I was a mess. Now I also had PTSD.

I remember my sister being there every day. I remember trying to play Connect Four one night but losing every game to her. Thank you morphine. I remember her crawling in bed with me one night and her crying on my shoulder. I knew she was super stressed but relieved I was still around to be a pain in her arse. She had to keep an eye on staff for me and I know she had trouble with a particular tech a couple nights, but I don't remember a thing. I know there were nights I cried in pain and she took care of finding the nurse to ask for more pain meds.

Coworkers and friends were incredible. I know I was out of it and slept a lot, but it seemed like there were always visitors or always fixing to be visitors. Every time I woke up, there seemed to be more flowers, stuffed animals, cards, or food. People took care of me, and also my sister.

Now my sister had a prior reputation here due to things she had pulled on previous visits out here. A bunch of shenanigans and not good shenanigans. So upon her arrival, she was taken aside and told basically to behave. She was told that if she was out here to help and be here for me, then she was very welcome. But if she was going to cause drama and be a problem, then she could hop back on the plane and go home. To this day, she's still upset about it and tells me she wasn't exactly welcomed by my friends. I've told her that they were taking care of business as they saw they needed to, and I was unable to do anything about it. Not that I would have changed anything anyway. But she was extremely helpful and was there for me.

The time came to figure out who I was going to go home with. I remember being given a choice of three different people, but somehow the choice was made for me anyway. I don't remember how that happened. I found myself going home with Cleo and Patricia. They were coworkers who I thought truly cared about me.

At first I thought it was grand. Cleo would take me to my many therapy and doctor appointments. Patricia would take care of me at home. I wasn't allowed to do laundry or cook or do dishes or anything. They kept telling me my job was to rest and get better. I tried to take naps and rest in my room, but I'd get yelled at by Cleo to get out of there and come out in the living room to be among people. I was exhausted. As time went on, I felt more and more exhausted. I didn't sleep well. I was awake many hours in the night. The medications weren't helping, and we were still trying to find the correct meds.

Slowly I noticed things the clearer my head felt. I felt closed in like I wasn't allowed to leave. I felt like I had to ask permission. When someone came to visit, I was judged for who my friends were. When a friend came to pick me up for a few hours out, I felt like I was judged then, too. If I posted something on Facebook in the middle of the night, Cleo told me I shouldn't post in the night because then people will see the time stamp and make assumptions. But in reality, they couldn't control what I posted in the night because they were sleeping. When I did something they didn't like, Cleo would have a "big brother chat" in the truck on the way to whatever appointment I had. I began to feel like I couldn't do anything right.

I really wanted to leave but wasn't sure how. I began looking for an opportunity. Miss Lilly became sick and went into the hospital. Her heart was out of rhythm. She was seriously sick this time. As always, she was worried about her cat, Bootsie, and wanted me to come and stay with her so I was on it. I stayed there several days. Meanwhile, I was getting grief from Cleo and Patricia. They wanted to know what my plan was. Miss Lilly had already told me that when I was well enough to be semi on my own, that I needed to move in with her. So I told the two that I was going to move in with Miss Lilly since she needed me with her health issues and such.

Oh, how they were pissed. But they didn't show it for exactly 2 weeks. They loaded up my things and brought it to the Vinita station. Then I got it from there. I gave them a thank you card with a $100 bill. I told them to go out for dinner or something. Now I had extremely little money. So $100 is really like $1,000 in this case. Exactly two weeks later I got text messages from them.

Cleo's text message:

"I've thought long and hard about this recently and it's been extremely hard for me to not say anything but it's just not who I am to keep my mouth shut. I'm highly irritated with you because of how you have made Patricia and I feel. A simple conversation with us on what your intentions were as far as staying in Vinita would have gone a long way. I'm still wondering how long you would have left us hanging if Patricia wouldn't have said anything. You had Patricia go for a drive with you and then all of a sudden you're gone without saying a word. It made me feel like you were taking advantage of Patricia's generous heart and that irritated me. I'm going to be extremely protective over her and I have bit my tongue because of our friendship but more than that out of respect for Patricia. The other thing that is eating at me is how it's like Mick didn't even exist. For the longest time after the incident, you stood up for Mick and what happened. You made the comment more than once that you loved and still do love Mick more than anything. Then all of a sudden out of nowhere, it's like he never existed. Do you not know or care what has been said about you and Henry being all lovey dovie. I'm not saying that you should just curl up in a ball but to me it looks like just because Henry is showing you so much attention then it's "Mick who". He was like a brother to me. I'm not excusing what happened but it still hurts with the impression you have presented. And now you're considering going after Mick's family. You said that would NEVER happen and now out of nowhere you're looking at doing it. Patricia did so much work to find a way to help you with bills and everything but that's not enough. I don't understand that at all. I'm not going to say anything else because I don't wanna get juiced up/pissed. You know for a long time before you and Mick got together you knew who he was. He was a kind man who would do anything for anyone and it just seems to me that you may have forgotten that. It's all good though. You have the right to feel however you want."

Patricia's text message:

"I thought long and hard about this and I wasn't going to say anything because well I'm just not the kind of person but I consider myself your friend and Cleo and I were here for you from the very beginning and for several months when not many other people were at least not in the way that we were. We were by your bedside almost every day and we took you into our home and we helped you no questions asked nothing in return. We pushed you, we were there for whatever you needed. Then one day you're gone not really much of a word as to what your plans were until I asked you which hurt especially after everything. We were honest with you always and up front, we never lied to you about what was going on. You kept telling people you were a prisoner here how do you think that made us feel??? We talked long and hard about mick and what possibly could have happened but it was said by you as well as us that mick loved you and that he was the love of your life, and you told that to many people. So my question is what changed? Why would you go after his family, his life he left behind, his grandchildren???? For money??? They had to put up a go fund me page to pay for his funeral. That's why we found that place in Oklahoma City that was going to help you with your medical bills and whatever else. What happened was tragic, yes, but you have become a stronger person because of it and you're alive!!! I'm sorry I just don't understand"

How do I even respond to that? How do you respond when you know that most of it is all lies? Do you bother to respond or just let it be? Do you ignore it and go on or do you stand up for yourself? Well, I took a moment to stand up for myself. Right or wrong, Mick and I were close and given more time, we would have started dating. That's as close as it was though.

My response:

"I seriously appreciate everything you and Cleo have done for me. I've never told anyone that I felt like a prisoner and I'm sorry it was taken that way. I joked on and off FB that they'd have to have Cleo's permission to kidnap me for the day, but it was meant as funny. Nothing else. As for what my plans were, I didn't really know. Just knew that Miss Lilly needed my help. Then moving at that time just happened that way. As for Mick, I loved the man he portrayed himself as, not the man he truly was."

I also emailed Patricia multiple times asking her if they had been receiving "hush money" from his family. I asked if that was the real reason they were so upset. I would think that if you take someone in to help them, that when they reach the point that they can move out, you would be happy for them. Not horridly pissed off. There has to be an underlying reason for them being so angry. I asked her multiple times. Every single time she ignored answering the question. His family has also been extremely hateful toward me, but more of that in the next chapter. When you refuse to answer a simple question multiple times, your action answers the question for you.

There were so many other people I could have stayed with. But now I know why Cleo and Patricia insisted I stay with them and why they were so angered when I left. It's truly sad that money was involved and that it ruined what I thought were good friendships. It's truly sad when someone allows money to ruin their perception of reality and make false accusations about someone. It's truly sad that someone would allow money to tarnish their vision and ruin their joy of life. I'm truly sorry things ended the way they did and wish it hadn't. I don't know how I could have done it differently though. I really don't. When someone is in the hospital, you don't know what will happen day to day. I wasn't sure what I was going to do until the moment Patricia asked me. It was my "do or die" moment. I've tried several times to explain things, but it's fallen on hardened ears. I still wish things were different. Maybe someday they will be.

Chapter 22

His Family and Former Coworkers Response

What you have

You don't know what you have...

Until you don't have it anymore.

When your hearing is greatly lessened,

When your brain suddenly doesn't work like it did yesterday,

When your medical issue list suddenly multiplies,

It changes your life.

You don't know what you have...

Until you are forced to depend on other for everything,

When you are not allowed to drive,

When you have no regular income to pay bills,

When you cannot be your precious independent self,

It changes your life.

You don't know what you have…

Until you have been through hell on earth,

When those you thought cared turn their backs,

When your life is severely threatened by someone you thought had your back,

When you struggle every day to appear normal,

It changes your life.

You don't know what you have…

Until you survive something that doctors fully expected to kill you,

When everything you are now capable of doing is something to be grateful for,

When you know that each person in your life is there because they chose to be by your side in the awful darkness.

When you are shown so much care, thoughtfulness, and love every single day, it absolutely changes your life…..moments at a time.

Live for those little moments.

Moments of humor.

Moments of love.

Moments of being able to do something you couldn't yesterday.

Moments of being able to truly smile through the tears.

Moments of having the opportunity to inspire others by your actions and reactions to your circumstances.

Moments of being inspired.

Moments of being amazed at how all your necessities are being taken care of from the physical to the mental to the medical.

Moments of joy at being able to hear the birds without straining to listen.

Life is one moment at a time.

Live life one moment at a time.

-BonniferWW

How would you respond if the person's family who tried to murder you came out and absolutely hated and despised you? What would you do if they tried to spread incredibly despicable rumors and untruths about you? How would you handle former coworkers suddenly coming out and turning their backs on you? What then? Just a heads up that this chapter will be a mess and may be difficult to read.....kind of like the ending of the last one. I didn't give you fair warning on that one though, did I?

Well, his family hated me from the beginning. In the hospital, I begged and begged to be allowed to go to the funeral but Patricia and Cleo would not allow me. They just kept telling me "no", but never explained why. I even told them I'd have an awesome ambulance service to transport me there and then back to the hospital. Still they refused with no explanation.

When I was discharged home and received my new phone replacement, I saw the message on my Facebook messenger. It was from one of Mick's family's friends. It stated that I was not welcome at the funeral and told me to refrain from attending. Oh it pissed me off.... even though the funeral was long passed. I was one of his closest friends and here I was being told that I was not allowed at his funeral. GRRRR!

Then on February 26th, 2018, his sister Sara messaged me on Facebook and stated, "It's been a little over a month, can you really not shed any light on my brother's last hours?" I replied with "Why would I talk to you when his family has only been rude to me? No one has asked me 'to shed light on his last hours'. No one has asked me how I am recovering. He fucking tried to murder me! I have absolutely nothing to say to any of y'all." Yes, again I was extremely pissed off. Imagine that.

After one of my news interviews had aired around November 25th, 2019, a person named Jenna commented "The part that saddens me is that the truth of the story has never been aired! Bonnie conveniently leaves out that she was having an extra marital affair with the man who shot her and continues to harass the true innocent people that were affected by this tragedy! This woman is a conniving monster who by no means needs praise!"

Now that comment is interesting because it has so much untruth in it. There was no affair going on. Mick lived a double life, but we already talked about that. There has been no harassment on my part. I have never initiated contact with these people.

A former coworker who was never at the hospital, wrote this on her personal Facebook page after an article/news interview. "She has done this to herself! We were the first there since this happened. What people need to know is she walks and runs w/o a Walker. Shes FINE! She has stolen, wrote mic hot checks after he died, gotten has ass fired from EMS bc she lies and steals money. What shomeone needs to do is call the news, tell all the 20 different stories that's she cant seem to tell the real story. And really stop feeling bad for her bc she is using people and pulling this shit for people to feel bad for her. This story makes me laughter bc what she says happened NEVER happened. But here we are...people feeling bad for her! Go investigate and you will she she lives a normal life, no limitations nothing! Then when its news time. THis is what she does!!!"

Sorry that is difficult to read, but it is written exactly the way she wrote it. Ugh! Anyhow, apparently according to her, the shooting never happened and I'm just making this up. I sure wish that were true. I wish that making up a story was my only issue. But I'm not making up any stories and it is ALL true. She needs to come spend a week in my shoes. I also did not get fired from EMS or any of the other accusations.

When I saw that, I messaged her and asked her if there was something she'd like to say. She said "Yes! Tell the truth." I told her that I am.

She replied with "Apologize to Patricia (inserted 2 laughing faces) you hurt her bad! Mercy, mic family and pay back the hot checks along with everything else you've done. It's not ok! It kills me to know what your doing! I thought you were a better person and it's so sad! You need help! And to be honest! You are fine! Its horrible! The truth will shine! "

I replied with. "Y'all sure like to make up stuff."

She replied, "Lmao oh girl...your a mess!"

I said, "Mick stole and forged a check. Have the documents to prove such. I haven't written a check since. Go read the police reports. The things that happened are not made up. Everything I have stated is the damn truth. I wish none of this bullshit had happened. Maybe if Mercy had better mental health concern for their employees, maybe things would have been different. Maybe if Mick hadn't been a liar and been living a double life, maybe things would be different. I am not going to explain my issues and life as it is now to fools such as you. Good luck."

I've also since found out that there are two Mercy employees, that were close with Mick, who Mick told he was going to commit suicide. This happened a couple weeks prior to the shooting. Guess what these two did? Absolutely nothing. Nothing!!! Plus a person in management is out telling other services about this. These two, at the least, should be helping me financially. But I am better than that. No wonder former coworkers were stirring the pot and spreading rumors. No wonder they seem like they are out to get and hurt me. They are feeling guilty. But just think, they really have Mick's life on their hands. They seriously do. They also have my life on their hands. All my health issues and all of what I have been through are on their heads. They should be paying for my expenses. They should be giving me money to live on right now since I've been turned down for disability. They should be begging at my feet asking what they can do to make things right. Yep! But I don't ever see that happening. Miracles still happen.

Now what do I make of this? When I heard this, I was instantly angry to be frankly honest. Angry because someone that I thought cared about me let someone else attempt to murder me knowing they were seriously suicidal. How could you? As time passed and I calmed down, I began to feel sorry for these two unknown people. Sorry because they are horrible and miserable and guilty souls. They have to live with what they did for the rest of their lives. If they would come and admit to it, they would feel much better. It still angers me, but I'm alive and I feel much sorrier for them than for me. They have a more horrid life than I do. I love them and I'd love to talk to them.

Now for my sister, she began posting things on her Facebook that made assumptions about my health. She claims she can tell when I'm having a bad day "without even talking to me."

How does she know? Because her "chest hurts and just the way I feel." Uh okay. This is not the whole twin thing. The set of twins have to be semi-close for that to happen and we are not close at all. Then here is what she said one day on her Facebook page when she was mad, "If you are the praying type, please pray for Twinny. It isn't a physical issue, but a mental and spiritual one. Not saying anything else here but thank you." This is because I didn't agree with her on my treatment plan. She told me my treatment wasn't working and I wasn't healing fast enough. I laughed so hard. I didn't know there was a timeline I was supposed to go by. I didn't know anyone was on a timeline. This isn't like someone with a broken leg.

Now, my sister wrote a very nasty letter to me. Before I ask you to read it, let me explain something. She is writing from a place of lack of understanding of what happened to me. I believe she's still in the stages of grief but doesn't realize it. She refuses to go through them. I died that day, but she still wants and expects me to be 'that' Bonnie when she no longer exists. I can only be the me I am today... the right now. To be completely honest, I have not read the letter. While typing it here will be the first time I read it. It reads…

Bonnie,

You think I do things for attention? You wear your WW shit and do races for attention. You contact Dr. Phil and others for attention! No, I didn't let you shave my head for attention. I did it because I wanted you to know that I'm here for you and I love you. I don't post shit on Facebook for attention. Maybe it would help you get disability if you posted your ER visits on your Facebook. Or maybe you should start making plans to survive if you don't get it.

I've done things for total strangers, but you don't know about it because I don't talk about it. I've done things for you but made it look like it was from people. So don't accuse me of things that aren't true.

If you want to judge and criticize my life choices, then be my guest. But I don't answer to you. You've been in plenty of bad places too. Those are your choices. I don't rub it in your face. Was rape even real? But that's between you and God. I don't care either way. I love you and I'll be here for you, but you will not treat me like the piece of shit you have for years.

I'm done discussing my trip there. I had a good time even if you were miserable. Miserable is totally your choice. Be ungrateful and self-centered. I don't give a shit. Miss Lilly wants me to come visit. Would be nice to see you for lunch or something if you don't still have that stick up your ass.

You want an apology? I'm sorry I spent so much time and money to help you deal with life, stuff for Princess, stuff for fun, and stuff you needed. I'm sorry I wasted a trip out there a few months back. I'm sorry that you are so ungrateful, pissy, angry, and selfish to realize the universe doesn't revolve around you. I'm sorry for what you've been through and that you obviously haven't been able to deal with the numerous losses. I'm sorry you got involved with someone who wasn't who he said he was and who planned your death. I'm sorry that you aren't grateful to be alive and see each day as a gift and a second chance. I'm sorry that you are hateful toward me. I'm sorry that you chose to not believe the truth. And I'm sorry that I've allowed you to treat me like shit for most of my life.

I'm still here for you, but do not contact me in any form unless you are ready to be a kind, compassionate, caring about something outside your universe, treat me like you treat your friends human being. I love you and always will. But I'm done with your shit!

-Yoana

Such love! I decided to write her a note and send a card. Now, as I already said, I did not read the letter until today. I received this letter May 7th and I just now read this letter October 1st.

Yoana,

I know you're hurting inside and angry right now. I get it. You basically lost your twin sister that day. You might still be grieving the loss of who I used to be. I don't know. You basically lost your identity of who you and "Bonnie" had been for 40 years. All of that was literally taken away in two gunshots.

I just now read your Oct 1, 2020 letter. I do nothing for attention. I do races to encourage myself and others. I also do them because it's what keeps me going. It's what keeps me sane. As for the wonder woman part, you seem jealous :)

I think we need to start over. I don't know who this person is (me) and am still very much getting to know her. Many days I hate her and wish I wasn't her. Then I realize (again) that she is me and I need to keep putting one foot in front of the other.

I'm asking let's do this together, not "across the road" or "miles apart" or however else you want to look at it. I don't know what the picture looks like, but we can figure that out as we go - even get help if we need to.

Anyhow, message me or something something.

Love,

Bonnie

There isn't much to say after words like that, except that I do hope she contacts me, and I do honestly hope we can get help. As for the coworkers and his family, only time will tell what happens. Hopefully, all good comes from this. I hope it's all good. Hopefully, the evil is over.

After a little bit of time, Yoana did contact me. We have been talking since then. But we've decided to leave the past and not discuss it. It is left untouched and unfixed. But at least we're talking now. I'll take it. Maybe someday, down the road, we can work on the actual relationship.

Chapter 23

Anger and My Response

Many Times It Is Sometimes

Many times, I don't know how to explain my emotions,

Sometimes, I need to be sad.

Sad that my old path in life will be no more.

Sad for time away from a career I loved.

For it's like grieving a great loss.

Many times, I don't know what to say,

Sometimes I need that still, quiet, and calm space

Where nothing has to be decided or done.

Where there are no cares or worries.

For, at times, words are not needed.

Many times, I am deeply angered.

Sometimes, I am angry at the one who caused this.

Sometimes, I am angry at myself for trusting and giving of myself so much.

Who can I trust again?

Who will love me for who I am now?

For, at times, anger is the only emotion I know.

Many times, I am seriously scared.

Sometimes, I worry about what my future holds.

Sometimes, i feel like my life will never have a sense of normalcy.

Will I always have to heavily depend upon others?

Will I ever be able to again hold a decent job?

For, at times, all I can see is what my life once was.

Many times, I am overwhelmed by the love and care given me.

Sometimes it is by complete strangers.

Sometimes it is by those who have stuck by my side.

Will I always have this multitude around me?

Will I someday be able to pass it on?

For, at times, it is this love that carries me through.

Many times, I am trying my best to be positive.

Sometimes, it is impossible.

Sometimes, it is like the wind beneath my wings.

Will I be able to continue seeing the silver lining?

Will I be able to mostly avoid the negative?

For, at times, I struggle to find anything even slightly good.

Many times, I feel extremely discouraged.

Sometimes, I think "something's got to give".

Sometimes, it is one minute at a time.

Will I ever be able to sufficiently support myself?

Will I ever not have to fight for what I need?

For, at times, it seems there is no end in sight.

Many times, I am completely exhausted.

Sometimes from disappointment or stress or pushing myself hard.

Sometimes from physical therapy and other appointments.

Will I ever have normal physical energy?

Will I ever not have so many medications?

For, at times, it all seems never ending.

Many times, it is sometimes that I feel that I will make it through.

Many times, it is sometimes that I feel strong.

Many times, it is sometimes that I know things will work out.

Many times, I am in awe of the fact that everything I have needed has been provided.

Many times, I am speechless at the support that I have going through this.

Many times, saying "thank you" seems so inadequate.

Every time, in my darkest days, y'all are there with me.

Every day, whether good, bad, or ugly, y'all show me I am loved.

Every day, my future becomes a teensy bit brighter.

Every day is a new day to become better, stronger, healthier, and more independent.

For every single day is a day that you didn't know you had.

For every day is a special gift.

For every day is something to value and be thankful for.

Every. Single. Day.

-Bonnifer WW

I'm going to tell y'all something here. After writing that last chapter, I struggled last night…..as in dark rough struggles. I also had the major physical pain aka horrible headaches to go with it. I had a rough night to say the least. I kept telling myself that if I can help someone else through the writing of this book, then it will all be worth it. I talked to a friend early this morning because of the rough time. She challenged me to take today as a self-care day, but also to make a list of things for which I'm especially thankful for today. So even though it's off chapter topic, here you go......

Today.....

I'm thankful for friends who listen in the darkest moments.

I'm thankful for being alive.

I'm thankful for my enemies.

I'm thankful for those who love me.

I'm thankful for life.

I'm thankful for my walker.

I'm thankful for my evil trainer.

I'm thankful for races.

I'm thankful for friends who do those races with me.

I'm thankful for Wonder Woman.

I'm thankful for bus rides.

I'm thankful for those who help me as needed.

I'm thankful for Mayo clinic.

I'm thankful for those who hate my happiness.

I'm thankful for my half a brain.

I'm thankful for pickles.

I'm thankful for my therapist.

I'm thankful for my new ability to write.

I'm thankful for my hearing aids.

I'm so thankful for so much in my life.

Okay. Now where were we……..

I'm not even sure of where to begin. I know that initially, outwardly I was asking questions about him like if he has suffered at all when he shot himself or about the funeral. I was saying that I loved him. I did love him. I loved the man who he portrayed himself to be. I didn't love the monster he really was. Even though I appeared concerned on the outside, the anger was slowly building on the inside. I initially felt confused. I had never experienced this ginormous turmoil of emotions before. The emotional roller coaster. How can someone say "I love you" but then shoot you trying to murder you? How can someone say "I love you" but then leave you knowing that you will probably die there alone before anyone finds you? How does that happen?

I talked to Patricia a lot because she was there at home with me the most. I don't remember the conversations, just that we talked and that I felt better after we talked. But slowly that anger built. I felt like I was expected or supposed to remain "sweet Bonnie" when all I wanted to do was go between crying and screaming and back to crying again. I felt like I was supposed to somehow just "forget" all the anger. But no, I kept it inside. I cried myself to sleep most nights. I cried most days when no one was home. I cried a lot because it was safe. It's what I knew. It's how I knew to deal with emotions and turmoil. But it still didn't get rid of the anger. I still felt like I wasn't supposed to be angry at Mick.

Why? He had tried to murder me! He had tried to fucking kill me! Who wouldn't be mad at their almost killer? Somehow Cleo and Patricia talked me into not feeling that way almost like it was wrong of me to be. They never said it was wrong though. Hang on, I can't think of the right words here. It was almost like every time I began to feel angry; they would remind me of the good times or something like that. The emotions would calm back down for a little bit. I felt guilty for having them. Of course I had no clue the emotions were being caused by the head trauma. I had no clue that it was totally okay and normal to be despising his guts. I had no clue that the ups and downs of emotions are completely normal with traumatic brain injury.

I was told that while I was still in the hospital, I was still crying for him. I said that I missed him. Well, I also know that while in the hospital, I did not know what was going on. I still have no recollection of many things that happened. This is besides all of the drugs I was being given. Traumatic brain injury people. Traumatic brain injury.

I don't remember when the exact moment was, but if I had to guess, it had to have been around the time that I tried going to do light duty in the office at the hospital. My anger was growing and rightly so. I began to talk to a few people I could trust…. the education officer being one. Then the owner of the company took me across the hall and introduced me to his personal lawyer. He had told me that whatever happened was none of his business, but that I needed to talk to a lawyer.

Prior to this, I had texted Patricia to update her on things such as appointments, life at Miss Lily's, talking to a lawyer. Wait! Yes, talking to a lawyer. She and Cleo were angry about that. They claim I promised to never talk to a lawyer which I have absolutely no recollection of either. First why would you make someone promise that? If you have to make someone promise that there's probably a reason that person should be talking to one. Then, why are you going to make a TBI patient promise anything? They aren't going to remember it.

When I was taken and introduced to the lawyer, it really did make me giggle a bit inside. Here was Patricia's boss basically telling me that I needed to talk to a lawyer. If she only knew, she'd probably pass out or shut up or go off on him. One of the three.

Yes, I was angry, and it was finally being able to be released. Not in outrageous ways.... I hope not anyhow. I tried to avoid that. But being able to talk to a lawyer was a relief in a sense even if they told me they couldn't help me. It was like a verbal hug. They'd point me in a direction to try or someone else to talk to.

Some religious people will say one of two things: one is that it's a sin to be angry at God or two is that they've never been angry at God. So first off, while it may or may not be a sin, it is definitely human nature to be mad at the one who is in control and could have magically stopped a situation. Like the Superintendent who could have stopped a school shooter or the parent who could have kept a child from getting hurt or the first responder who could have saved a life if only they were there sooner. It's human nature to blame whether that blame is legit or not. Second, to say that one has never been angry at God is a flat out, big time, major lie. That's like a teenager saying they've never been mad at their parents. Or siblings have never fought with each other. Or someone has never ever gone over the speed limit, not even a hair for even a split second. Right! And I have ocean front property here in Oklahoma for sale too. Would you like to buy it unseen?

Was I mad at God? Hell yeah I was. We had major long talks and discussions where many times I did all the talking. Sometimes I did most of the talking. Other times, I let him have a word or two. Ha! Do I feel like I "sinned"? Nope! Why? We are emotional souls, and we were/are made that way. We are unable to be healthy and unemotional. It is not who we are. Can you imagine talking throughout your whole day monotone, no emotion, no anything? All day, every day, your whole life? Nope, surely not me.

Am I religious? NO! NOPE! And hell NO! Do I believe in a higher being? Absolutely I do! I wouldn't still be here today without one. So it is that higher being that I refer to when I say God. To me, it is about a personal relationship with him/her, not some man made up religion.

I was angry. I was very depressed. I drew within myself. I trusted only a few people. I thought everyone else was out to get me and destroy me. I wanted to just hide in the corner and not deal with people. I wanted to stay in bed. I wanted to punch the wall. If HE was still alive and of course in prison, I wanted him to be in a very small cell with a TV on playing a replay of what he did to me over and over and over again. This would replay for 24 hours a day 7 days a week. I told my therapist this once and she agreed with me.

I wished there was a way to bring closure to this. I wished there was a way to tell his family to leave me alone. I didn't cause this and I'm not bothering them, so let me be. For a long while, it seemed that every time I turned around, his family was causing me trouble or attempting to anyhow. Nasty notes from various family members and friends, then his daughter leaving horrible comments on my pictures on Facebook from several years ago. So many things.

I searched for months for a purpose for why I was still here and around. Why did I survive all of this? Why was I still suffering? Why was I still being tormented? Why were some of my closest "friends" turning their backs on me? Why was my parents ignoring me now of all times?

You raise me up.

You raise me up

When my world is crashing.

You raise me up

When my life is in shambles.

You raise me up

When others turn their back.

You raise me up

When all I see is darkness.

You raise me up

When I am sinking fast.

You raise me up

When some only try to spread negativity.

You raise me up

When I don't have the strength for one more step.

You raise me up

When no one else is watching.

You raise me up

When I am dragging.

You raise me up.

When my sight is too blurred with tears to see.

You raise me up

When my heart is crushed.

You raise me up

When the bad and rough news is overwhelming.

You raise me up

When there is no end in sight.

You raise me up

When those I thought I knew choose a different path.

You raise me up

When I am ugly in temperament and personality.

You raise me up

When I am unlovable.

You raise me up

When others would have given in.

You raise me up

When all hope is gone.

You raise me up

When my darkness turns to thrashing storms.

You raise me up

When no one is listening.

For without you, I would not be on the brink of another
sunrise.

Without you, I would not have the energy to reach another
sunset.

For it is you that gives me hope and strength that sunshine is just around the bend.

-BonniferWW

Chapter 24

Growth Through Despair and Darkness

The Dark Day

It's a dark day.

I feel like it can't get any darker.

But then it does.

I keep falling.

Deeper. Farther down. Deeper.

Down this dark never-ending hole.

Falling farther...deeper...darker...

How much farther does it go?

When will it stop?

How much more must I endure?

Falling farther...deeper...darker...

Why does it have to hurt this bad?

Why am I the one chosen to bear this?

Why do I have to suffer?

Falling farther...deeper...darker...

Why must I suffer for someone else's choices?

I didn't ask for this.

I only tried to help someone I thought was a friend.

Falling farther...deeper...darker...

My heart aches.

My head hurts.

My mind never slows.

Falling farther...deeper...darker...

When will the nightmares end?

When will the flashbacks stop?

When will my life return to "normal"?

Falling farther...deeper...darker...

So many medical appointments.

So many medications and pills.

So many feelings, thoughts, and emotions.

Falling farther...deeper...darker...

What else must I lose to the person who decided my life wasn't important?

Privilege of driving.

My car.

My career.

My independence.

People I thought were friends.

Family.

My joy.

My smile.

My belongings.

My ability to trust.

EVERYTHING!

My life is forever changed in some form

Unknown yet how much or in what permanent ways.

Someday there will be light.

Someday the falling will end.

Someday I will see the full purpose in my suffering.

But that day is not today.

Never give up.

Never give in.

For its five minutes at a time.

-BonniferWW

Have you ever been at the end of your rope? Like
legitimately at the end of your rope? Have you ever been so
far into the darkness, that there was no light? It was darkness
into darkness. Or have you been so far deep down into a hole
that you felt like there was no way back up? You felt like the
only way was down?

Yes I've been there. I've had that plan. I looked up on the
internet how much of what medications (I currently had at the
time) I'd have to take to end it all.......and do it for sure on the
first attempt. I've been on too many ambulance calls where a
patient had been suicidal, had done his method correctly, but
because he was found, his life was saved. I wanted to have
the right plan for when the time came.

Yes I was in therapy. My therapist's name at the time was
Lauri. She worked at a well-known facility in Tulsa. At the
time, I was receiving no psychiatric drugs, not even
antidepressants. I asked her what I needed to do to be

prescribed them. She told me that I did not need them currently. Uh excuse me? I don't ask for them unless I feel like there's something wrong or I'm heading in the wrong direction.

When she had this response, I went straight to my family doctor. I told him what had happened. I told him that I thought I needed to be on them because I was starting to struggle. He very much agreed to put me on them. He also explained that it was very normal for what I had been through and what I was currently going through.

The following several weeks, I went slowly deeper down the hole. I mentioned it to my therapist that I was now on antidepressants. Her response? She was suddenly glad that I was on them and said so. WHAT? What happened to the thought that I was okay without them?

I mentioned that I was falling down the hole and struggling to which she told me that I was doing really well and blah blah blah. When I continued, she finally said she'd refer me across the hallway to the psychiatrist. FINALLY! When I tried to make that appointment, it was still three months off. THREE months! How was I going to make it another three months? I seriously didn't think I could. When I told Lauri this and that I didn't think I could wait that long, her response was "Well, they're really busy over there." I asked her if she could do anything to get me in quicker. She replied with "No. They are really busy over there."

I was only seeing my therapist every two weeks, so it was rough and hard work to make it that long. At this point, I reached my lowest point ever in my life. I hadn't ever been this far in and this low in the darkness ever before. I was scared what I would do. I was scared of what my therapist would do, but I had to tell her. That day, I walked into her office and flat out told her that I was scared. I also told her that I had looked up on the internet for the doses of the drugs I had at home to see how much I'd have to take to end it all. Her response? Absolutely nothing except to say, "You are doing so great Bonnie!" Really? Here I am begging you visit after visit for help. Now I'm pouring my guts out with honesty about where I'm at and all you can do is completely ignore what I just told you, be completely disrespectful of me, and be the most incompetent therapist I've ever known or even known about. I should have been checked into the hospital for help.....not sent home. What if I had attempted suicide that night? What if I had been successful? My attempt or success would have been on her head.

I left her office in horrible tears. Julie was sitting in the waiting room waiting for me. I immediately told her we had to talk in the car where I told her everything that had happened in the office. We talked and decided we'd call Family and Children's Services right after physical therapy since that was next. I felt so much better after letting it all out and telling Julie everything. I hadn't told anyone how bad things had really gotten.

The next week, I found myself at Family and Children's Services filling out all the intake paperwork. Julie was with me again. The staff was kind and caring. The following week I met with my new therapist. She was an older lady with a kind heart and a big listening ear. I told her what had happened to which she was utterly shocked. We talked more about me, about the incident, about her life and experience. It was like an hour spent with an old girlfriend. Soon the time was up and time to say goodbye until next time.

That hole is an extremely horrible place. If someone comes to you and says they are in that spot, please listen to them. Please help them. Please be there for them. Not just then, but later too. If someone says they are going to hurt themselves, hurt others, or they have a plan to do either, then they need help. Your job is to get them that help. Take them to the hospital. Sit with them in the hospital room. If you can't do that for whatever reason, call 911 at the very least. If Mick's family had called 911 that day, he may not have committed suicide that day. If my two former coworkers had reported that Mick was suicidal those two weeks prior, I may not have been shot in the head. Mick may not have committed suicide. If you refuse to help someone who is suicidal, then their actions and outcome is your fault.

Now, if he hadn't had done what he did, I wouldn't be where I'm at. I wouldn't be receiving the blessings that I am currently. I wouldn't have the purpose and drive I now have. I wouldn't be writing this book and my nickname sure wouldn't be Wonder Woman now would it?

Even in the worst moments come the greatest possible joys. Even in life's nightmares come the best fulfilled dreams. For in the darkest moments comes the brightest light.

Never broken!

Some say I am broken,

Broken to the core,

Too broke to repair.

Some say I am broken,

Broken with no hope,

Too broke for anyone to care.

Some say I am broken,

Broken with no way out,

Too broke to ever return.

Some say I am broken,

Broken to be broken for forever,

Too broke for anyone to Love.

Some say I am broken,

But since when did I listen to what some say,

Too broke to ....pffffffff!!!

I may have been hit, but I am not broken.

I may have been knocked down, but I am not broken.

I may have been discarded, but I am not broken.

For I am still alive. Still breathing. Still thinking. Still healing. Still loving. Still me

I will rise again,

Stronger.

I will love again,

More confident.

I will trust again,

More independent.

I will run again,

Better listener.

I will live again.

Better discernment.

Despair? Agony? Pain? Absolutely!

Living and loving life in the way I'm able? Absolutely!

Anger? Hurt? Depression? Absolutely!

Learning difficult life lessons? Absolutely!

Broken? Never!

Love me in my darkest hour and I will always be there.

Despise me in my roughest moments and I will never look back.

Love me in my fight against the grim reaper and I will always fight for you.

Despise me when I need you the most and I will never need you in my life again.

 But broken? Never!

 -BonniferWW

Chapter 25

Purpose for My Life Now

Your Purpose!

The more you shine, the more a few will try to make it stormy.

The brighter your light burns, the more a few will try to squelch it.

The more positive you are, the more a few will try to blow the negativity out of proportion.

The more you seek to encourage others, the more a few will try to discourage you.

The more you rise up after falling, the more a few will try to keep you down.

The more you continue to wear your smile, the more a few will try to make you scowl.

The more you be yourself, the more a few will try to change who you are.

The more you use your situation for growth, the more a few will try to stunt that growth.

The more you continue plodding forward one foot in front of the other, the more a few will try to divert you from that path.

The more you stand tall, the more a few will try to make you stumble.

The more you learn about your new purpose for being here, the more a few will try to make you feel worthless.

The more you begin to live for your new purpose, the more a few will try to take your purpose from you.

The more you begin to love every moment in life, the more a few will try to convince you of how selfish you are.

The more you let those few bother you, the less time you have to live to your fullest potential.

The more you let those few steal your focus, the less time you have to focus on your purpose.

Look forward.

Love big.

Live life.

Stay focused.

Be strong.

All at 5 minutes at a time.

-BonniferWW

Why did I survive such a gory event? Why am I still here?
Why do I have to suffer for someone else's choices? Why do I
have to be made an example to others of being "too kind" or
"too this" or "too that"? Why do I have to go through such
pain... emotional, physical, mental, etc.? Why do I have to
suffer so? Why do I have to lose my ability to work? Why do I
have to lose belongings? Friends? Coworkers? Family? Why
did I have to lose everything I had? Why.....why.....why?

I asked those questions so many times. Sometimes to actual
people. Sometimes to myself. Sometimes to God. Sometimes
just to the empty nothingness that was. Oh how I cried when
I asked those questions. At times I still do, to be honest.

What is my purpose in all of this? I struggled with that for
months. Through everything I had been through in the last
many months, I still hadn't discovered it. Sometimes I
thought I had. People kept telling me, "You need to write a
book". I knew I wanted to do that, but it didn't seem like a

purpose yet. Plus everything was a complete wreck in my head. I could barely form a sentence without it being a mess sometimes. How would I write a complete book?

I thought, "Well, maybe it's public speaking," but I couldn't even talk straight. How was I going to talk to people for 20-30 minutes? It would be absolutely painful for them and just thinking about it, I felt bad for whoever would listen to me. Ha-ha!

Then I thought well, maybe it's to take care of Miss Lilly, but that quickly became clear that she didn't need or want me in that way. She would have major yelling fits at me for no reason. She had trouble with me not being the old me. She'd hold it in as long as she could, but then would explode. She'd be mad the whole day. I'd hide all day long.

I thought well, maybe it's to volunteer at the hospital and help out that way. Though it did help me feel useful and needed, it still didn't feel like it was my lifelong purpose. I enjoyed it greatly. I looked forward to it and did it when I wasn't struggling with health issues, but not my purpose.

I did a couple news interviews and thought to myself, "Oh that was nice." I was able to encourage some people. Maybe? Then Julie and I did a few races…. The Little Rock Marathon and Route 66 Half Marathon. There were some smaller races in there, but I don't remember those as much. Anyway, I had gone into these races doing them for me as a way to keep my sanity, doing something I love, have fun, and spend time with my Sidekick Julie. Now I walk these races using my wheeled walker…. all races - from a 5k to full marathons. I wouldn't be able to do them otherwise. But I began to realize that I wasn't there for me. I was there for other people. Random strangers would come up to us and share their own triumph stories from beating cancer to knee surgeries to traumatic injuries. There would be a horrible massive hill ahead. We'd push through it and climb to the top. Then afterwards, there was bound to be at least a few people that would come up to us and say that they wouldn't have made it up that hill if it hadn't been for us ahead. They realized that if we could do it, then they could too.

There were more news interviews. It seemed that every time there were interviews, there would be hate responses from his family or my former coworkers. Something usually happened. But as of late, they've chilled out.

As for my purpose, I began to realize that at least part of it was to be there to encourage others in many forms. In news articles, in TV news reports, and in races. I can't run and now have to walk so I'm in the back of the pack, but you know what, I see so many people. It's much more fun in the back.

Now hang with me as I tell you this. It may seem as long a topic as a rabbit trail, but it isn't. I had to change neurologists as the first one kept telling me , "You're only here for your seizures," even though I had many more neuro issues than just seizures. So on my first visit to my new neurologist, he put me straight into speech therapy. At first, I was like "say what? Speech therapy? How's that going to help my brain?" He said it would help the cognitive as in the unruly scattered thoughts. Then I was all about it.

I started. It was what would seem like elementary games on paper and flashcards. I grew extremely frustrated because I knew I should be able to do these things. But as time went on, it became a bit easier. Of course then my therapist, Juliana, just increased the difficulty level. But it was working. I could form sentences. I could think of the right words. I could have actual conversations. Sure, I still have issues and still stumble, but it's far better.

I had also told Juliana that I wanted to write a book someday about everything that's happened. One day we talked about my ideas for it.....how the chapters were going to be compared to the miles in a marathon; how it would start with the incident, then go into my childhood, then back to the incident, then finally looking to the future. I knew what I wanted to say. I just didn't know how to say it. One day she told me I was ready to start. I beamed with excitement. My first assignment was to write out the list of the chapters. After that, it was to write one chapter a week. But anyhow, the point of telling you this? Goals! You got this! You can do it my friend! Work through it. Stumble through it if needed. But you'll get there one step at a time.

So now I know that one part of my purpose is to be here to encourage others, to carry others as I am able, and to be a listening ear. I have a friend who calls often to talk. She also has PTSD and anxiety due to it. She's also had a stroke. She told me that she calls me because I understand her. She knows she can ask me anything. I'll be completely honest with her. I wouldn't be available to talk with her like I am now if all of this hadn't happened. I'd be too busy working and taking care of other adult responsibilities that happen in the normal adult world.

Another purpose is writing these poems. I don't know why or how, but I couldn't write poems before the incident. I had tried many times but failed miserably. Suddenly afterward, I could write. Instead of writing in a journal like normal, I wrote poems. It just flowed out that way. I've been told that my poems have helped people, too. Now I can't just sit down and magically write out a poem. It pops into my head at the right moment. Then I have to immediately write it down. Otherwise it will be forever gone. I sure won't remember it. Crazy brain of mine.

Whether the public speaking happens down the road or not, I don't know. But for now, I'll keep doing the races. Yes, they do keep my sanity. But they also cover a huge purpose for being here. It's a big responsibility, honor, and privilege really to be able to do this.... walker or not. If you're a runner, walker, or soon to be one, I hope to see you out there on the course. A big fist bump or hug is waiting for you.

Just the way you are!

I love you

Because of who you are

Because of who you were

Because of who you will be

But most of all, I love you just the way you are.

I love you

Because of your strength

Because of your tenacity

Because of your courage

But most of all, I love you just the way you are.

I love you

Because you are human

Because you have weaknesses

Because you know when to ask for help

But most of all, I love you just the way you are.

I love you

Because you feel emotional

Because you feel exhausted

Because you feel enough

But most of all, I love you just the way you are.

I love you

Because you make me feel

Because you make me live

Because you make me laugh

But most of all, I love you just the way you are.

I love you

Because you have always been there for me

Because you have always listened to me

Because you have never given up on me

But most of all, I love you just the way you are.

I love you

Because of that sparkle in your eye

Because of your zest for life

Because you lend a hand

But most of all, I love you just the way you are.

You could be younger or me older.

Me dumber but you wiser.

You empty, but me more fulfilled.

Me a bum, but you on 5th Avenue.

You a scholar or me a professor.

Why are we here then?

Why am I reading this?

Why have you penned this to me?

Why? Because whether you are reading this prior to much life experience or after or even somewhere in between, I want you to know one very special little thing:

No matter what you do,

Whether you be rich or poor,

No matter where you go,

Whether you be well known or known not at all,

No matter who you become,

Whether you be homeless or not,

No matter what trouble you cause,

Whether you have a career you love or a job you despise,

No matter what good you help do,

Whether you run for president or town mayor

No matter what sorrows you face,

Whether you end up in jail or die on death row,

No matter what accomplishments you gain,

I love you just the way you are forever and ever!

-BonniferWW

Chapter 26

Life now, goals, and new meaning

A Superhero's Cape

Not all superheros wear capes.

But all superheroes have mementos.

Some good. Some bad.

Some beautiful. Some ugly.

Nor are all capes worn by superheroes.

Not all superheros wear capes.

But all superheroes have assistance from others.

From a child to a granny.

From a storekeeper to a physician.

Nor are all superheroes visible to the naked eye.

Not all superheros wear capes.

But all superheroes have big hearts.

Showing love to those who others have disposed of.

Giving strength and hope to those who so desperately in need.

For showing others what life is meant for.

Down deep, in the deepest parts of a superhero, lies the love for others.

Down deep, inside a superhero, he has his own superhero.

Down deep, inside the home of a superhero, hangs his cape. Shhh!

This cape?

What! Superheroes wear capes?

But you just said…..!

Yes dear one

Not all superheros wear physical capes, but all superheroes do have "capes" in how they have helped others.

This superhero?

I will always carry my cape…

For the homeless man sitting in the rain.

For the mother trying to carry groceries home to her hungry children.

For the sick child in need of comfort.

A cape is not always a piece of fabric, but a heart, a hug, and a huge listening ear.

-BonniferWW

Have you ever had a time where you were forced to make a major life change? As in there was no opportunity to go back to the way things were yesterday? But today, you are homeless or today you are fired from your job or today your house burned to the ground or today ………..? What did you do? How did you handle it? Did you lay around thinking

"Oh woe is me!" or did you pull yourself up by the bootstraps and go at it to figure it out? Well, maybe both huh? Maybe not.

Throughout this whole recovery process, every time there was a moment to begin to panic, things were taken care of. A while back, I didn't know where I was going to live because my money was getting low. I worried and I fretted. I asked around if someone needed a roommate.....who couldn't pay rent but could help around the house as I was able. Zero response. I asked around for someone who could keep an eye on me and let me live with them. I had some maybes, but that was it. Then I remembered an offer I had even farther back from Sam and Lorna. They had told me that if I ever needed a spot to live that I was welcome to come stay with them. I called them up and asked if that offer was still good. You know people.... sometimes they say things but hope you forget or they don't really mean them type of things. Lorna told me the offer was still good. YES!!!! It was a major load off of my shoulders.

I've been living with them since the end of February (7 months at the time of writing this). It's been grand. My doctors and therapist are even happy that I'm living with someone who's responsible and all. They're happy because I'm not trying to live on my own anymore. Stupid falls and all you know. But it's been a very grand decision I've made to live with them.

Per my doctors, I am not allowed to live alone because of my falls and passing out. I have issues with this because my blood pressure will randomly drop in the 60's systolic over

30's diastolic. That's as low as my cuff will read anyhow. I still have to use my wheeled walker to walk very far.......doctors say more than 30 feet. I have major severe headaches that I deal with every day. I still have cognitive issues. I have issues related to PTSD.....a lot of issues. I suffer from depression and anxiety. I have frequent nightmares. The list goes on. But in all of this, I've learned to keep trudging forward, to let others help carry the load, and to allow yourself to ask for help as necessary.

My dreams and goals? Sure, they've changed a bit. I can't ever go back to work as a paramedic again. That's a given. So those goals and dreams are probably not going to happen. Are they lost forever? Don't know yet, but for now they are on the far back burner. But like running races.......I can no longer run them. I can walk them though with the walker. I may never place in my age group because I can't run fast, but I can sure walk fast and show the world how it's done being a walker. Just because you are forced to change directions doesn't mean that all your goals and dreams are lost. You may just have to change how you accomplish them.

Yes, I have many issues, but it is in how you view them and what you want to do with your life. Yes, I have my very bad and horrible days where I can only stay in bed and I have many of them. Yes, I have days where all I do is stay in my pj's, cry, eat potato chips, and sleep. I have those days too. I have days where I'm so exhausted but have a day full of appointments. That makes me cry too. I have those days. We all do.....some figuratively. Even Wonder Woman is human.......THIS Wonder Woman! I can't see straight, I can't hear you, I can't run, I can't do a lot of things. (Sounds like a depressing country song. Now I love country, but not the depressing mess.) But you know what? I'm here right now, right here, talking to you. Yes you! Right there, YOU. It's completely okay to have a bad day. It's also okay to wallow in our troubles and sorrows... for a minute or three. But please do not stay there. It can be a very very dark place and if you stay, it can become difficult to leave. Get help if you need to. Talk to a friend. Call 911 if needed.

As for goals and dreams? They can change and grow. When goals change, plan new ones. Meet them next. When your dreams fade, dream bigger and follow them. My goals? My goal is still to live life past my health issues. No matter which ones I deal with the rest of my life, live past them and don't let life stop me. Another goal is to help encourage as many people as I am given the opportunity to. Whether it's through walking races or public speaking or something else, I know it's my purpose through this to be here still. Another goal is keep learning to love my family and those who I would love to strengthen my relationships with. I would love to have a chance to seriously workout whatever the issues are with my parents and my sister.....probably with mediators though. Face to Face. Pure honesty.... if that's possible.....from all parties. I think that would also qualify as a dream too. I would love to be able to have an adult level of a mother and daughter relationship. I'm currently working on my relationship with my sister. Maybe something incredible will happen. Something incredible only experienced by twins. Another dream is to be able to travel first to the states, but then the world. I'd love to be able to complete either a half or a full marathon in every state. It would be amazing to participate in other countries too. Another dream is to be able to help other TBI patients obtain social security disability and other much needed resources quickly, also to make sure that families are automatically told about these resources upon admission. I want to have a way to make sure that these patients have help at home and for the long run, not just in the hospital. There is so much more I could go on longer.

I used to sit at home in between my work shifts and wonder, "Does my life have meaning?", "Will I do this job for the rest of my life?", "Is my life the example I want it to be?", "What will I remembered for when I'm dead?". I thought about these questions and others often. When that person looks at me - like really looks at me, what do they see? A villain? A saint? A liar? A friend? Something else? What? But then who do you ask those questions to that would seriously give you a honest straightforward answer? A spouse, relationship partner, friend, coworker, cafe employee, passing stranger? Who would you ask a super-duper personal question like that to? Hmmm.

Instead of figuring out those questions, you suddenly find yourself in a completely different world where you are forced to depend on others, where you can't hear normal, where you have frequent nightmares, and where you have multiple health issues. Your world, life, goals, dreams, and attitude all change. Many more things change than thought possible. It sure changes your outlook on life. Life is precious. Life is worthwhile. Life is tough. Life is rough. Life is everything.

This all has given me new meaning and purpose to my life. Now compared to back then doesn't even compare to my meaning of life. Then I thought it was to be a Paramedic and save lives on the ambulance until I retired or hurt my back. But now, I know it is sitting here writing this while chatting with you, my new friend.

Chapter 26.2

P.S.

Choose to be grateful!

I could cry

I could scream

But instead I choose to be grateful

For I still have my wits.

I could hide

I could lock the door

But instead I choose to be grateful

For I still have my strength.

I could stay in bed.

With the covers over my head

But instead I choose to be grateful

For I still have my love for life.

I could be a hermit

I could never be seen in public

But instead I choose to be grateful

For I still have my love of people.

I could be a bum

I could be a bitch

But instead I choose to be grateful

For I am still very much loved.

I could never try

I could give up caring

But instead I choose to be grateful

Because I don't know how to quit.

I could say it's gotten too rough

I could say it's not fair

But instead I choose to be grateful

Because I still have much.

I could stay in the darkness

I could stay inside my head

But instead I choose to be grateful

Because I have far too much to live for.

I could easily focus on all the negative

I would have every right to

But instead I choose to be grateful

Because I have been able to help so many.

I could easily stay focused on myself

I could forget all around me

But instead I choose to be grateful

Because I wouldn't be here without those who are around me.

-BonniferWW

Wow! 26.2 miles! You've almost read a marathon! Ha-ha! If you're trying to read this chapter first, then please go away. You're still loved, but you need to start at the beginning. You got caught! Okay okay. You can read this chapter first if you insist, but the mystery lies inside. Just saying.

If you've made it this far, I just want to say thank you. Thank you for caring enough to have the desire to pick up this book. You are awesome! I do hope that you've enjoyed it, but also that you've found encouragement through reading it.

This chapter is my designated chapter for me to say to you whatever else I feel or think I need to say before I end this book. Just because this book ends, the story does not end. It's nonstop forward.

We all face intense and horrible challenges. It seems completely unbearable inside the worst moment of it. And it is unbearable. I've been there. That's when you need to ask for help. It may be finding food resources or a job or counseling. It may be making yourself go to the emergency room to get help. I've mentioned suicide a few times here. Please do not. You are worth it. You are worth it to me. You are why I wrote this book. For you. YOU!

On the other side, be there for your friend if they need help. Watch out for each other. Help them when they ask. Help them when they don't want it. Listen to them. If you need someone to talk to or assistance with resources, call 411 in your area and they will be able to tell you what is available and help you get what you need.

I could live life pissed off mad at the two former coworkers who did nothing when Mick told them that he was going to kill himself. I could forever be mad at his family members who he told on the day of, that he was suicidal. I could be bitter at Cleo and Patricia for their treatment of me and for not getting me the help I desperately needed. The list goes on. The thing is, living that way would only make them win. It would only give them joy. It would only give them pleasure in knowing that they helped to ruin my life. That's me stooping to their level. That's me giving up. That's me letting the devil and the Grim Reaper win.

FUCK NO!!! That will not happen! I will rise up. I will take life the way it has been handed to me, and I will fight hard with everything I have. I will give it everything I have. I will not let anyone win. This is my life, and I will live it proudly and accomplish things that others told me were impossible.

You can do this too! Don't let others' words control what you accomplish in life. Do not let others' opinions of you control how you think of yourself. Don't let people tell you what you are or are not going to do. If you can dream it, you can do it.

If you have a disability or a hardship or something in the way that someone is telling you that is the reason why you can't do something, you can still get it done. You can still live that dream. You just need to figure out a different way of doing it. Like my races…. I can't run them anymore, but I can walk them with my walker. There's always another way. Don't let a disability or hardship keep you from living life in whatever way you choose. You got this. Big hug!

Ya'll, you mean so very much to me. I wouldn't be sitting here right now if it wasn't for you. In the hospital, I fought hard. At the house, I fought hard. At Miss Lily's I fought hard. Even now I continue. Do you know what gives me courage and strength to keep going? You do! Each one of you. I'm not just saying that either. It isn't just random words filling space on a page. I mean it. It's you. Y'all have been so amazing and so encouraging through this. Complete strangers…....you too. Your words and actions. Your hugs and prayers. Your love and trust. All I can say is thank you. Thank you for being there. Thank you for carrying me through this. Thank you for being my strength. Thank you for being you.

I sure wouldn't be A Wonder Woman without YOU. Go show someone you love them. Go take a homeless person to lunch. Go pay a stranger's electric bill. Go pay the car behind his/her fast food bill. Do something special for a child or an elderly person. Tell a veteran "Thank you". Write a card to military personnel who are overseas. Send a care package too. There are many things you can do to be a superhero. Those are just a few suggestions.

Now go be a superhero too!

Made in the USA
Columbia, SC
13 February 2021